CAPITOL STORY

A DREAM OF THE NEW ALBANY.

SCRIBNER'S MONTHLY—DECEMBER 1879

EXCELSIOR

CAPITOL STORY

by CECIL R. ROSEBERRY

with photographs by ARTHUR JOHN DALEY

*Stained-glass windows
in Assembly Lobby impart
a faintly ecclesiastical
touch to a political
scene. Inset figures
are Peter Minuit
and DeWitt Clinton;
State Seal at the top.*

EDITORIAL COMMITTEE
General C.V.R. Schuyler, *Chairman*
Hugh M. Flick, *Editor-in-Chief*
Mildred Ledden, Isabelle Savell, John Moore,
Mason Tolman, George Wiesner
Murray Belsky, *Art Director*
CONSULTANTS
Albert B. Corey, *State Historian*
Charles S. Kawecki, *State Architect*

Library of Congress Catalog Card
No. 64-63030
Published by the State of New York
Copyright 1964 by the State of New York

STATE OF NEW YORK
EXECUTIVE CHAMBER
ALBANY

NELSON A. ROCKEFELLER
GOVERNOR

FOREWORD

The State Capitol at Albany is an extraordinary building, a repository of some important chapters of our history, and rich in irreplaceable architecture of a bygone era.

Hemmed in for decades by row houses, it is reemerging today as one of the focal points of a great new redevelopment project, on which the State of New York and the City of Albany are cooperating, to create a fitting capital for the Empire State. It is therefore doubly appropriate that its colorful history should be published at this time.

In compiling this volume, the editors and staff were extremely fortunate in having the unstinting assistance and counsel of Dr. Albert B. Corey, who served New York State as its Historian for nineteen years. As the book neared completion, Dr. Corey prepared the cogent introduction which follows this foreword. It proved to be one of his last services to the State he had served with such ability and devotion. Tragically, on November 10, 1963, he succumbed to injuries from an automobile accident. "Capitol Story" is therefore, in a very real sense, a memorial, and a fitting one, to this distinguished public servant, whose work over the years enhanced the lives of all the residents of the State.

"Capitol Story" is an absorbing narrative. It adds a colorful and significant chapter to our State's history, and is certain to elicit new appreciation and understanding of a unique building, the Capitol of the Empire State.

Nelson A. Rockefeller
Governor

INTRODUCTION

No one is ever lukewarm in his opinion of the Capitol in Albany. Either he looks upon it as an atrocity of jumbled architecture or he enjoys it as a successful blending of architectural forms which is esthetically pleasing. Perhaps those who dislike the Capitol are architectural purists who demand that a building follow a single style from foundation to roof or they believe state capitols should have domes. Since objectors are much more vocal in their dislike than those who approve, the approval, which is quite as sharply but less vociferously expressed, is sometimes drowned out.

This book has been written not to redress the balance between the two but to tell the story of a building which is unique among state capitols in the United States. It took thirty years to build, it is the product of three groups of architects, and it cost far more than any other capitol. It is so solidly built that Civil Defense authorities are hard put to find any shelter that exceeds its protective qualities.

The Capitol was begun in an era when European forms still dominated the design of public buildings in the United States. It was completed a score of years after the age of structural steel had begun. The thirty years between the end of the Civil War and the turn of the century witnessed a wave of expansionism, experimentation and innovation throughout the country, and nowhere more so than in New York. This ferment affected industry, business, government, education, and the arts. Old forms were not discarded completely, rather they were changed and modified to express the cultural needs of the time. It is into this framework, as an expression of an age, that the architectural variations of the Capitol must be placed to be understood and appreciated. The Capitol is a symbol of an era when change was in the air.

The compelling quality of this book is that the author, drawing on a wealth of contemporary sources of fact and opinion, has written a critical, objective, and yet sympathetic story of the Capitol. It leads to an understanding of Lieutenant Governor William Dorsheimer's statement in 1876 that the building should be "A school of architecture in itself to the people of the State."

ALBERT B. COREY
State Historian

1. CHATEAU ON A HILL

Winter withheld its cold breath that year as if purposely to help along the hurried work of finishing the new Capitol. Crews labored in day-and-night shifts. They would have been working Sundays, too, except that some pious organizations protested.

At the Christmas season of 1897, the unlovely sheds of stone-cutters and masons came down. Rubble was whisked away. The premises were raw and muddy—no walks, no landscaping. But the people who owned it could finally get a clear look at the fabulous structure on the hill for which so much of their tax money had gone. There never was such a building!

New York State's Capitol as viewed from the west. This is considered its most sophisticated façade. The roof line and dormers especially create the impression of a French chateau of Francis I period.

The reason for the sudden haste was the determination of Governor Frank S. Black to walk up the 77 steps of the Eastern Approach on the first day of the new year and open the front door. It would be a symbolic public act, and at the same time give him a great deal of personal satisfaction.

For almost twenty years the state government had been operating without a front door—ever since the old Capitol was vacated. The new Capitol had been in gradually increasing use during that time, though incomplete. Access had been gained via side entrances not yet dignified even by porticoes.

Governor Black had vowed to finish the Capitol during his term. In his inaugural message to the Legislature he had said:

"This subject may well be approached with reluctance. It is about 30 years since the building was started, and over $22,000,000 have been appropriated and spent or sunk. It has dragged itself through nearly a third of a century, always clamoring for money, until the people have nearly despaired of its completion and have come to regard it as an affliction from which time affords but little hope of relief. If an individual or a corporation had managed an undertaking as this has been managed, they would have been discredited years ago.... This building ought to be finished at once. The work should be done by contract, and sufficient money appropriated to pay for it. The State needs the structure for its uses, but it needs still more to escape the scandal of a building of enormous cost and unparalleled extravagance undergoing at the same time the process of construction at one end and decay at the other."

At the end of his first year in office, the Capitol was not yet finished but the end was in sight. The superb front flight of steps—almost the final touch on the exterior—was done, except for some carving.

The construction of the gigantic pile had been the dominating factor of Albany life since the Civil War. A whole generation had grown up since it was begun. It had taken as long to erect as the Great Pyramid of Cheops. It had cost twice as much as the national Capitol at Washington. Tempests of controversy had swirled around it. Long before it had reached this stage, its fame had spread throughout the world. Travelers came to gawk at it, unfinished as it was. Magazine pieces were written about it. A Governor had gone so far as to call it a public calamity. Friendlier observers saw it as "the most interesting public building in the country." It was the expression of an era of American life. It was a veritable school of architecture and museum of stone-carving.

Without much fear of contradiction, it could have been said that nowhere else on earth was there a building in which architecture and politics had been so closely intertwined. In one instance, the style of its architecture actually had been legislated!

It had another uniqueness: it did not look as a Capitol was supposed to look. Almost by unwritten law, Capitol buildings in the United States had domes. This one was conspicuously domeless.

The monumental, rather overpowering, heap of granite at the top of the rise from the Hudson River had somewhat the aspect of a New World castle. This was accentuated by its whiteness. The light-hued Maine granite so carefully selected for its exterior was as yet unsullied by atmospheric grime. The plateau on which it stood was 150 feet above the river's tidewater, and the face of the building rose more than 100 feet still higher. The imposing effect was magnified by the fact that the city as yet had no other tall building to compare.

Instead of a dome, this unconventional Capitol bristled with red-tiled turret peaks and steep roof ridges. Its skyline was restless with handsome dormers and tall chimney stacks. The style of its architecture might take some untangling. But the roof features gave it one valid and striking architectural comparison—that is, to a French Renaissance chateau of the reign of Francis I.

The building had been a steadily growing problem for ten governors before Governor Black inherited it. Ground was broken under Reuben Fenton, and John T. Hoffman laid the cornerstone. John A. Dix and Samuel J. Tilden watched its walls rise. Lucius Robinson so detested the building that he refused to move in when its first wing was opened, and thus it remained for Alonzo B. Cornell to be the first to use the executive suite. Reform-minded Grover Cleveland tried to speed things up by putting an expert builder-architect in complete charge, without the usual Capitol Commission to confuse matters. David B. Hill fought to keep that official's hands from being tied, and then sweated through the so-called "ceiling scandal." Roswell P. Flower signed appropriations with the refrain that "the wisest economy now is to complete the building." Levi P. Morton instigated a private-contract system instead of day-labor, but had trouble getting it rolling.

Frank S. Black, a prosperous lawyer from Troy, was a tall, spare individual of scholarly mien. A gift for oratory wafted him into politics almost without his own

Eastern Approach stairway
as it looked when new,
with potted palms
and ornate electroliers.
Governor Frank Black
walked up it to open
front door for first time.
At right: George W. Aldridge,
public works superintendent,
who pushed the building
to completion by order
of Governor Black.

volition, and when the Republicans ran him for Governor in 1896, one of his campaign promises was to finish up "that building" on the Albany hill. Soon after his election, the *New York Tribune* said editorially:

"There are two things which the State Capitol at Albany may confidently be relied on to furnish: an enduring opportunity to spend large sums of money, and an occasion for speculation as to when, if ever, the huge pile will be finished."

Governor Black quickly got an agreeable Legislature to abolish the existing Capitol Commission and to transfer its powers to the State Superintendent of Public Works, who was then to complete the Capitol "by contract." There happened to be still in office a Commissioner of the new Capitol, Isaac Perry, dating from the Cleveland administration. He was not eliminated, but he was placed "under the direction of the superintendent of public works." In other words, the "grand old man of the Capitol," as Perry was affectionately known, went into partial eclipse at the end.

The superintendent of public works who now took charge was George W. Aldridge, an experienced building contractor from Rochester as well as the aggressive political boss of Monroe County. When Governor Black told him to get the Capitol done, no matter how, Aldridge said: "I will do the work or break my back."

The contracts Aldridge awarded contained a stipulation that the Eastern Approach staircase and the main entrance must be finished before January 1, 1898. Hence the hectic work with the day-and-night crews. The abnormally mild weather was a godsend. It didn't seriously snow until the last day of the year.

On New Year's morning, Albany awakened to the season's first sleigh bells. One of the cheerful vehicles drove Governor Black, in mid-forenoon, up to the Eagle Street margin of the undeveloped space that would be Capitol Park. There a select group of state dignitaries awaited. Superintendent Aldridge had laid a plank walk across the frozen mud to the foot of the staircase.

The Governor alighted and stood for a moment, letting his gaze travel over the impressive white façade of the building, now so entirely exposed. Perhaps he was remembering that when the ground was broken for it, he had been a boy in short pants, living in Maine at no great distance from the quarries whence came the bulk of its granite. Now he was a man in his mid-forties and, by the curious workings of chance, had risen to the highest office in the state which built it.

Governor Black then led a small procession across the planks, up the middle of the staircase, and in through the groined arches. Beside him walked, on the one hand, Superintendent Aldridge; on the other the Governor's son, Arthur. The Attorney General and his staff followed, and then the heads of various other State departments. The march was flanked by a squad of police guards.

At the New Year's reception ensuing in the Executive Chamber, Governor Black accepted plaudits, and the talk was mainly about how fast the work on the Capitol had been done in the past nine months.

To the incoming Legislature, Governor Black said: "There will be no further alteration. The structure will be completed, the sheds torn down and the walks laid out, before the first day of next October. There has not been a time in the last fifteen years that reasonable effort would not have accomplished these things in twenty-four months."

The Spanish-American war flared that summer. A special session of the Legislature was called to decide how New York should play its part. In spite of this interruption, the Governor kept his promise about the Capitol.

There was a picturesque charge up San Juan Hill in Cuba. The hero of it returned home to be elected Governor of New York. Theodore Roosevelt was the first Governor to take the oath in the finished Capitol.

Turn-of-the-century photo, found in an Albany attic,
shows Capitol when it was new. The Tub was hotel popular with lawmakers.
Al Smith stayed there as young Assemblyman.

2. THEMIS DETHRONED

The old Capitol was a hat-box compared with the new. Meekly it stood while the granite bastions of its successor grew behind until they shut off the afternoon sun. The shadow was prophetic of doom. A journalist said the condemned relic "seemed to crouch at the feet of the new edifice"; that it looked "diminutive, humble—almost mean."

New York's earlier Capitol had the aura of a frayed, decrepit, but beloved antique. Its only real virtues were a four-pillared Grecian portico and a dome that was more accurately a cupola. Affixed to the flagpole above the portico was a "time ball," electrically controlled, which dropped daily at the stroke of noon. And perched atop its dome was a wooden statue of Themis, 11 feet tall. Themis was the Greek goddess of divine justice, accoutered with a pair of balances and a sword. The city literally looked up to her.

One eery night, shortly before the old Capitol was scheduled for the wrecker's hammer, a thunderstorm toppled Themis. She crashed to the sidewalk, barely missing a belated pedestrian. Some people speculated that Themis did this as a gesture of protest at the injustice of it all.

Nostalgic tears were shed over the building in which such Governors as DeWitt Clinton, Martin Van Buren, and William H. Seward had presided; which had played so major a part in the rise of the Whig Party; where Lafayette had been lionized and Abraham Lincoln had spoken. Reviewing its past, a newspaper mourned: "It was a liberal education in the political history of New York to know the old Capitol."

For all the gush of sentiment, nobody went so far as to defend it on the score of utility or architectural merit. The truth was that the original Capitol was skimpily built and that the most opulent state in the Union had long since outgrown it—was even a trifle ashamed of it.

The Grecian portico gave the Old Capitol a classical flavor, but the cupola atop was distinctly Philip Hooker. The city looked up to wooden statue of Themis, the Greek goddess of divine justice. For 70 years, the currents of New York State history flowed through these pillars.

Albany became the capital city almost by accident. New York had been the seat of colonial government. When the British captured that city, members of the provincial assembly, firearms in hand, met in various Hudson Valley towns. The fugitive "capital" shifted from Harlem to White Plains to Fishkill, then veered between Poughkeepsie, Kingston and Albany. After the Revolution, the Legislature continued to "meet around." New York and Albany competed for the honor of becoming the permanent capital. In Albany, the sessions were held in the ancient Dutch Stadt Huys, which served as city hall and courthouse.

ALBANY STADT HUYS

Government breeds records and documents. It became decidedly inconvenient to transport the necessary papers back and forth. When it met at the Stadt Huys in 1797, the Legislature passed a bill for erecting "a public building" at Albany for the storage of "records, books, papers, and other things." This building, known as the State Hall, was by no means a Capitol—but it meant that the Legislature was putting down roots in Albany.

The proposal to erect a "state-house" in Albany came to a head in 1804 when the city offered to donate a lot on its Public Square, and also to shoulder part of the cost in return for sharing its use. The Public Square was a well-trodden open rectangle at the top of State Street hill, long used as a recreational and parade ground. It commanded a pleasant view of the sail-studded Hudson and the rolling hills beyond. The Legislature accepted.

A favored way of raising public moneys in those days when taxable resources were sparse was the lottery. The State did not hesitate to resort to the gambling instinct to help pay for its first Capitol. The cost of the building was $110,685.42. Of this amount, $32,000 was raised from the lotteries.

The cornerstone was laid in 1806 by Mayor Philip Schuyler Van Rensselaer, a son of the Patroon, Stephen Van Rensselaer. While the building was going up, Robert Fulton moored his steamboat at the waterfront below.

There chanced to be in Albany a designer of buildings, Philip Hooker, who already had a wide reputation. He was given the job. Hooker had learned his profession from his father, and was what might be called a practical architect. His style was to be greatly admired in future years as typical of "American classicism." The only one of his buildings that survives intact in Albany is the Joseph Henry Memorial (originally the Albany Academy), which stands near the present Capitol.

The Capitol built by Hooker faced squarely down Albany's broad central thoroughfare to the river. It was more impressive by virtue of its location than by size. The Ionic portico gave it a flavor more Grecian than "American classic." But the cupola-dome was distinctively Hooker.

The building was occupied in 1809. Not just the State moved in—but the mayor of Albany, the City Council, and the Board of Supervisors. By the sharing of cost, the state, city and county had become bedfellows. This was an odd arrangement that could not last indefinitely. In 1829, the State bought out the city's interest for $17,500. Albany applied the money to erecting a City Hall—also, incidentally, designed by Philip Hooker.

Curiously enough, no law ever was passed designating Albany as the capital city The nearest thing to it was an 1809 act appropriating $5,000 "for the completion of the public building, which building shall hereafter be denominated 'The Capitol.'"

Agitation began as early as 1829 to relocate the capital city—preferably to the "geographic center" of the State. Utica and Syracuse were most frequently mentioned as possibilities. The Erie Canal had been dug, the railroads soon were spinning their web, and people flowed into the hitherto sparsely populated hinterlands. Cities like Buffalo and Rochester sprang up. Legislators from the western counties found themselves at a disadvantage in traveling to and from Albany.

Early sessions of a peripatetic Legislature were held in colonial Stadt Huys, Albany's city hall. Above: Congress Hall was famed hotel, neighbor of old Capitol, whose purchase by the city cleared way for the new one. So many legislators lodged there that it was virtually an annex to state government. At right: the cornerstone of first Capitol, preserved in wall of Western Staircase.

At the same time, dissatisfaction with the Capitol building grew apace. Even with the city out of it, expanding State activities stretched its seams. The chambers from the start were cramped and ill-ventilated. Committees were named to study its shortcomings. One of these reported that the Assemblymen habitually complained of "a dizziness in the head, accompanied by severe pain caused by the impure air thrown into the chamber."

When the Civil War was at its height, in 1863, Senator James A. Bell, from Dexter in Jefferson County, started the ball rolling for a new Capitol, with this:

"Resolved, That it be referred to the Trustees of the Capitol and the chairman of the committee on public buildings, to procure suitable plans for a new capitol, with adequate accommodations for the several purposes for which the same is needed, and to report to the next Legislature."

The chairman of the Senate's committee on public buildings was John V. L. Pruyn; Senator Bell was one of its members. In all probability, Senator Pruyn was behind Senator Bell's resolution, since he was a zealous promoter of the new-Capitol project long before it matured. Pruyn descended from the ancient Dutch aristocracy of Albany, was a bigwig in the Democratic hierarchy known as the Albany Regency, and the able attorney who drafted the incorporation plan of the New York Central Railroad.

An advertisement inviting architects to submit designs for a new Capitol was inserted in newspapers, over the signature of John V. L. Pruyn. Only three firms responded at that time, one being Fuller & Jones, architects of the new Parliament buildings at Ottawa, Ontario. Nothing came of these designs. No actual money rode along with the resolution. Obviously, the State did not intend to do anything more concrete about it until hostilities were over.

The case against the old Capitol was summed up by an Assemblyman from the floor: "Sir, when this building was originally completed, it was doubtless the most prominent and attractive feature of Albany. Dwarfed by its surroundings and depreciated by contrast, it has long since become an offense to the eye and a reproach to the State. . . . At an expenditure of more than one million pounds sterling, the Canadas have treated themselves with a Parliament House at Ottawa, the boast and fame of which fill the Continent. . . . It is said the State of New York is poor, and cannot afford to have a decent Capitol. Sir, I deny it. The State of New York is rich, and can afford to have a decent Capitol. One that shall fairly meet her wants, and correspond with her rank and power."

But should it remain in Albany? A select committee of the Senate was appointed "to ascertain by correspondence, or otherwise, with the city of Buffalo and other municipalities of the State, on what terms the grounds and buildings necessary for a new Capitol and public offices can be obtained." An inquiry was sent to all cities and more than 200 villages. Few took it seriously. Some replied with tongue-in-cheek humor, if not outright sarcasm.

The village of Argyle invited the Capitol on the score that: "It is a very moral and religious place, and can be recommended as a location on account of presenting no temptations to legislators to depart from the paths of *virtue*." The village president of Whitesboro wrote: "If the location of the capital of the Empire State is to be put up to the highest bidder, like the yearly State Fair or the poor-house of a county, then, and in that case, the village of Whitesboro is not a competitor." Buffalo, specifically mentioned, was not interested. The mayor of Utica skeptically responded that "any proposition we could make would not influence the moving of a *brick* from the present location."

New York City, Albany's rival of yore, was very much in the market. Its aldermen voted to make a site available in Central Park, at the Battery, or Tompkins

Square, or Mount Morris Square—and was ready to throw in a spot for an Executive Mansion on Fifth Avenue.

The Legislature had made its gesture. Albany had no intention of letting the Capitol get away. Its Common Council took a vote and notified the State it was willing to "purchase and convey to the State of New York . . . the block of ground known as the Congress Hall block, or any other lands in the city required for such purposes."

Congress Hall was a hotel which, by long usage, had become virtually an annex to the Capitol, the haunt of legislators and much used for their committee meetings in the absence of proper state-house facilities. The rambling hostelry stood between the Capitol and Washington Avenue. Its proprietor was a well-liked Negro, Adam Blake.

While neither the old Capitol nor Congress Hall stood on the actual ground desired for the new building, their locations would be needed for the broad Capitol Park in front. The site proper was mainly full of residences.

The Senate committee which sent the feelers throughout the State concluded that "to remove the Capitol from Albany at this time would not be justifiable, and from the character of the majority of the letters received, and the refusal of many cities and villages to reply to the circular of the committee, we think it cannot be desired by the people generally." The Legislature thereupon passed an act (May 1, 1865) stating that whenever the city deposited a deed conveying to the State the Congress Hall block, the Governor was to nominate three men to be designated as the New Capitol Commissioners, "for the purpose of erecting a new capitol." An allowance of $10,000 was made for the Commission to begin obtaining plans.

The city wasted no time in fulfilling the conditions. Congress Hall was purchased from Adam Blake for $190,000. It was left standing, however, until 1878, when Blake used the money to build a new hotel downtown, the Kenmore.

Reassured that the Capitol plan was really moving at last, Mr. Pruyn and John Bridgford, a local building contractor, bought up the residential properties needed. Pruyn turned his over to the State without recompense, while Bridgford sold his at cost. (Bridgford later became the first superintendent of construction on the Capitol.)

Governor Reuben E. Fenton appointed as the three original Commissioners: John V. L. Pruyn, by then a Member of Congress; Hamilton Harris, also an Albany attorney; and Obadiah B. Latham of Seneca Falls, a long-time construction man. The Commission then chose Hamilton Harris as its chairman. Harris was a brother of U. S. Senator Ira Harris, whose daughter, Clara, had been a guest in the box with the Lincolns at Ford's Theater the night John Wilkes Booth invaded it.

By an act of April, 1867, the Legislature appropriated $250,000 "towards the erection of a new capitol." The act stipulated that none of the money was to be spent until a plan had been adopted which was "not to cost more than four millions of dollars when completed."

Excavation began before the end of that year. A foundation stone was laid in 1869 with a speech by John V. L. Pruyn in which he said:

"Here may wise laws be enacted. Here may purity and integrity of purpose always mark the action of executive power. Here may justice, the attribute of deity, be inflexibly administered."

The old Capitol stood, however, until 1883. That August it came down. James W. Eaton was the executioner. Eaton had been building superintendent of the new Capitol for a number of years. Displaced by Governor Cleveland's appointment of Isaac Perry, Eaton returned to his private business as a construction man. He put in a bid of $1,000 for the salvage value of the old Capitol and it was accepted.

*John V. L. Pruyn was an influential
advocate of new Capitol, a member
of original Commission. His head
is carved on Western Staircase.
Hamilton Harris, an Albany attorney,
was chairman of same Commission.
On this page are depicted two rooms
in the Capitol that was abandoned.
At right: the Governor's Chamber.
Below: the Senate Chamber in use,
portrait of Governor George Clinton
on rear wall. The same painting
now hangs in the Executive Chamber.*

When old Capitol was razed in 1883,
the four Ionic columns were last to go,
standing mute guard over rubble (above).
Their ornate capitals were salvaged
and today grace the lawn of a country club,
Wolfert's Roost, as lower photo testifies.
Right: the prior Capitol in its final days,
with its successor rising to the rear.
Themis was still on her perch, defiant.
A point of criticism of Hooker's design
was the effect, created by windows, of two
stories on front, three stories on sides.

3. ARCHITECT NO. 1

Thomas Fuller was a Britisher who absorbed Victorian notions of architecture by studies in Bath and London, and built a cathedral on the West Indies island of Antigua. When he was thirty-four years old, in 1857, he fared forth to try his fortune in Canada. Luck sailed with him.

Landing in Toronto, he formed a partnership with one Chilion Jones. Canada was just then in the ferment of becoming a Dominion. Cities were vying to be its capital. Queen Victoria arbitrated the choice. With some diplomatic prompting, she gave the decision to a mere "hole in the woods"—a lumber settlement on a bluff by the Ottawa River. A design competition was announced for a cluster of Parliament buildings at Ottawa. Fuller & Jones entered, and won. The rearing of that stately Gothic group in the wilderness caught the popular imagination and vaulted Fuller into sudden renown. It also inoculated him with an ambition for grand public structures.

When it was advertised that New York State was contemplating a new Capitol, Thomas Fuller, then residing in Ottawa, began submitting designs. He was persistent.

The process by which New York arrived at an acceptable plan was long, involved, and frustrating for the architects who tried and fell by the wayside. Fuller & Jones first entered a design in 1863. When the Capitol Commission was formed under the act of 1865, it invited fresh designs and received thirty of them. Fuller, by this time in partnership with Augustus Laver, submitted a second design. The Commission reported in 1867 that "no one of said plans had on examination been found satisfactory." But it saw merits in one submitted by Arthur D. Gilman of Boston, and asked him to prepare a new one "in conformity with the instructions of the Board." When Gilman did so, it was rejected.

The legislation contained a joker. Any plan adopted by the Capitol Commission must also have the approval of the Commissioners of the Land Office. These latter were influential gentlemen, among them the Lieutenant Governor, the Secretary of State, the Attorney General, and the Speaker of the Assembly. They proved difficult. One thing they insisted upon was that the building must have a dome, or a central tower of some kind. The Capitol Commission itself was not so set upon this, and Gilman's plan did not have one.

In the course of events, Gilman and Fuller got together. Fuller's medium had been Victorian Gothic. Gilman was an Italian Renaissance advocate. An uneasy compromise resulted between Renaissance and Victorian Gothic. Fuller and Gilman joined forces and submitted a massive design that provided for a spectacular tower. Both commissions approved it. Governor Reuben Fenton put his signature to it on December 7, 1867, and ground was broken two days later.

By this time, Fuller's job on the high bluff above the Ottawa River was completed. The Dominion of Canada was a reality and Parliament had just occupied its buildings. Fuller now had found another hill, beside a tamer but more historic river, upon which to convert his dreams into stone. He moved to Albany to devote full time to the Capitol, opening an office in town under the name of Fuller & Laver. Gilman was allied for a time as a consultant.

The Capitol Commission appointed Fuller as resident architect at a salary of $10,000. It was customary for an architect to take for his fee a percentage of the cost of the building he designed. When the Commission cannily proposed that he accept the salary basis instead, he argued a little, but finally acquiesced. Had he been paid by percentage, it was estimated that Fuller would have received easily $250,000 by the time he was dismissed.

The Fuller-Gilman design was primarily Italian Renaissance, and therefore not in imitation of the Canadian Parliament structures. There were, however, some elements of similarity in the tormented skyline and the turrets with fancy iron grills on their roofs. How Fuller thought about the building is revealed in his first report to the Commission:

"In the exterior composition of the design there is a general adherence to the style of the pavillions [sic] of the New Louvre, of the Hotel de Ville of Paris, and the elegant Hall or Maison de Commerce recently erected in the city of Lyons. Without servile imitation of any particular example, the architects have produced a composition in the bold and effective spirit which marks the most admired specimens of modern civil architecture."

The plan was a conventional compilation, but it was what state officials and commissioners of the moment desired. The Land Office men had dictated the grandiose tower. Legislators indicated where they wanted their chambers to be. High-ceilinged rooms were much in vogue. The architects had to please many masters. As a matter of fact, Fuller showed himself amenable to changes as the work progressed. When the time came that he had to defend what he had been required to do, he was at least partially justified, it seems, in protesting: "I cannot but express my surprise that the report of the 'advisory board' should place upon me the entire responsibility of the adoption of the central court, the position of the main tower, legislative halls, the size of the rooms, etc., whereas they were called for by those in authority."

The transiency of elective officials was a disturbing factor from the start. Plans approved by one year's authorities might be disapproved by the next. Appropriations often were reduced. Such vacillations surely were enough to give an architect insomnia.

One of the three original Capitol Commissioners was openly critical of the Fuller-Gilman design. This was Obadiah Latham, the only early commissioner with actual construction experience. He dissented from his two colleagues in the adoption of the plan, and wrote Governor Fenton urging him not to approve it. He sent memorials to two successive Legislatures pointing out the flaws as he saw them. The Fuller plans, he said, were "not the best that were offered," and were "unsuitable and imperfect in important and essential particulars." For instance:

Main Parliament Building at Ottawa, Canada (above), brought fame to Fuller. It was Gothic in design and had real integrity. Comparison with his original plan for New York Capitol is interesting. Similarities in roof-lines are notable, though the Albany building was Italian Renaissance and far more pretentious.

"The leading idea of the arrangement of the interior seems to have been to secure a quadrangle, or open court yard, with a corridor surrounding it. This arrangement destroys the direct communications of the different departments." The plan deprived the building of what any Capitol was normally expected to have, "a grand central hall or vestibule." The external design showed "a want of harmony, and gives the effect of eight distinct buildings." Latham charged that his two fellow commissioners, Harris and Pruyn, were "proceeding with the building without consulting me." And he predicted rightly that the ultimate cost would "far exceed the sum limited in the statute for the completion of the work."

The Senate Finance Committee went through the motions of investigating Latham's complaints. The result was that the 1868 Legislature appropriated another $250,000 to go ahead with the building as planned, and even authorized making it bigger by the acquisition of more property—an extra half-block on the west side of Hawk Street. At the same time, the Legislature cautioned the Capitol Commission not to proceed any further if it began to look as if the cost would exceed $4,000,000. One is reminded of the mother who told her charming daughter she might go for a swim—"but don't go near the water."

If those delegates of the people appeared singularly unworried by the ample warnings about cost, it must be remembered that—in spite of the depression of the 1870s that quickly ensued—this was a financially free-wheeling era. The birth of the Capitol coincided exactly with the rise of the notorious Tweed Ring, and "Boss" Tweed was a member of the State Senate. The scandals of the Grant administration were soon to unfold. Even as the foundations were being laid, Jay Gould and Jim Fisk precipitated "Black Friday" with their plot to corner the nation's gold market.

William M. Tweed, having become the leader of Tammany Hall, deliberately had himself elected to the Senate in 1867 in furtherance of his scheme to gain control of the entire state government. In a lavish suite in an Albany hotel, he "held court" and dispensed his favors to law makers who were obedient to him. In 1868, with the help of gross election frauds, he promoted his New York mayor, John T. Hoffman, to the governorship. Political ethics hit rock-bottom in Albany. A Tweed biographer has said: "A more degraded Assembly than the one over which Tweed's Speaker presided is hard to conceive. There have been others more corrupt. But this one was without shame."

This, then, was the noxious political atmosphere amid which the Capitol project was undertaken. That "Boss" Tweed tried to get his fingers into the Capitol pie was strongly insinuated by John V. L. Pruyn at a later date when he had been dropped as a commissioner. "I was left off the Commission by Mr. Tweed," he was quoted in an interview, "for the reason, perhaps, that I was not sufficiently flexible for certain purposes."

In any case, it is perfectly clear that the Legislature itself gave the go-ahead after it was common knowledge that the $4,000,000 limitation was a dead issue although it remained on the books. When an Assembly subcommittee investigated the skyrocketing cost in 1874, it absolved the Commission of any blame. The commissioners, awakening to reality, had given their opinion that the cost would ultimately exceed $10,000,000; after hearing which (according to the Assembly committee's report), "the Legislature itself assumed all the responsibility for the plans of the building, and adopted the same definitely."

The construction operation began with a prodigious digging, after many buildings were razed. John Bridgford, who had helped to buy up the properties, got the excavation contract and was named superintendent of the job. Earth was removed by manual labor to an average depth of more than fifteen feet over an area of nearly three acres. It was "an extraordinary spectacle"—a continuous procession of 200 wagons "in close rank from morning to night," carting away the dirt to use as fill in nearby ravines.

The digging uncovered something that would persist in Capitol legend all down the years—quicksand. The site is underlain by a deep deposit of glacial lake clay. Laced through the clay were found several veins of sand which, when saturated with water, behaved like quicksand. In each case the sand was scooped out and completely replaced with clay or concrete. This was asserted in construction reports to the Legislature. But the specter of quicksand continued to haunt the Capitol. Every time something has gone wrong with the building, it has been blamed on that "quicksand."

As for building material, the original intent was to use native stone of New York State exclusively. A small granite quarry north of Saratoga Springs was given a contract in the hope that it could supply all the granite. The hope was soon dashed. Not only was the quarry inadequate to keep a large supply flowing, but the stone was not uniform enough in color. The services of Dr. James Hall, the state geologist, were enlisted to obtain granite samples. The commissioners themselves traveled to quarries far beyond the bounds of New York State. They finally decided upon certain New England granites because of their light hue and even texture, and contracts went to a quarry at Keene, New Hampshire, another in Maine. In the end, practically all granite for the outside walls and steps came from Hallowell, Maine. The quarry had the extra advantage of being near the seacoast, and so the granite could be cheaply transported by water.

The Commission leased wharves of its own at the Hudson waterfront to receive the granite. It made a contract with the Albany Railway Company, owner of the local horse-car lines, to haul the stone up the hill. A rail spur was run into the Capitol grounds. For many years, a familiar sight in Albany was the teams of draft horses, hitched in tandem, straining to draw a weighty block of granite on a flatcar up the stiff grade. The company kept three or four stand-by teams "to supply the places of those giving out."

"Whatever might be the superstructure," said an early Commission report, "the commissioners deemed it their duty, beyond question, to secure a substantial foundation." A four-foot mat of concrete was laid for the basement floor. The outside basement walls are as much as six feet thick. (In recent cold-war years, the Capitol basement was designated a fall-out shelter. Thanks to the fortress-like way those walls were built, the state is warranted in claiming it as one of the safest fall-out shelters in existence.)

Iron was not an important constituent in the earlier phases. Structural steel was a thing of the future. The solid brick arches of the basement are illustrative of the all-masonry method that prevailed. This building, in fact, spanned a transition period in construction practice. Only in the upper portions does one encounter steel i-beams. The Capitol was completed just as the skyscraper era was dawning.

The building was a major industry for Albany. Its payroll, when the masonry was going full blast, fluctuated between 1,000 and 1,500 men. In a sample year, the figure was 1,398, of whom 536 were stone-cutters. Cynics often referred to it as a "patronage factory." There is little question that politics sometimes played a part in the dispensing of jobs.

When the basement walls had risen to twenty feet, it came time to lay the cornerstone. This event occurred on June 24, 1871. The weather itself provided an augury of things to come. It rained all day!

Governor Hoffman, who radiated courtesy and dignity and was trying hard to live down his Tweed background, officiated at the ceremony. He did so with

Top-hatted figure at laying of cornerstone is presumed to be Thomas Fuller, architect. Photo of him in 1889 (right), from the Canadian Archives, bears a strong resemblance. Below: Governor John T. Hoffman who officiated at ceremony. Opposite: newspaper ad inviting architects to submit designs.

aplomb, despite the fact he had recently proposed that work on the Capitol be suspended while plans were modified in the interests of economy. Hoffman even had suggested that some of the "abundant space" might be used for the official residence of the Governor.

The cornerstone was prepared several days in advance at the northeast corner of the foundations. A cavity was cut in its surface to receive a metal box containing mementoes of the occasion. This basin was kept filled with ice water in the interim. It was a brief fad among the townspeople to go up and take a drink out of the cornerstone. A young man stood beside the stone with two dippers and ladled up the innocent potations. Visitors added a twist of their own: they tossed good-luck coins into the water.

Cornerstone day was to be a gala day in Albany. Thousands made long journeys to attend. But then, early in the morning, a cold, dismal rain began to fall. It kept coming in torrents with no let-up. After delaying as long as they could, officials finally gave the signal for the parade to start. It was a long parade, with brass bands and drill corps, and a large number of visiting Masons, since that fraternal order was to conduct the ritual. All who could get hold of umbrellas carried them, and a bystander was reminded of "marching toadstools." A large crowd defied the rain. A young man who went home and wrote down his impressions for posterity said: "The American flag endeavored to wave, as is its custom, but being wet with the rain it could only droop around the mast."

Thomas Fuller, architect, was on hand to be honored for his work. While the multitudes got drenched, the Governor and other main participants had the shelter of a canvas canopy on the plank platform.

Hamilton Harris, still the Commission chairman, presided. Governor Hoffman sidestepped saying anything specific about the building by confining his remarks to the history that had led up to it, starting with Henry Hudson. He concluded on the platitudinous note: "Let us lay the corner stone of our new Capitol with the prayer that our beloved State may continue to grow in the future as it has in the past."

Instead of passing around ice water, a workman kept sopping rain out of the cornerstone cavity with a sponge. The Governor lowered the metal box into it. Among the contents were copies of all legislation relating to the new Capitol, various U.S. coins and currency of 1871 mintage, and Albany newspapers of the prior day. The word went around that an Albany couple had postponed their wedding so that the notice of it would be printed in the papers going into the cornerstone.

Finally the Masonic order took over. Thomas Fuller was presented to the Grand Master, who handed him a square, level, plumb, and span, and said:

"Labor on this task, and be blessed, my brother, in the work. May it be blessed with Wisdom in the plan, Strength in the execution, Beauty in the adornment; and when complete, may Wisdom be still within its walls, to enlighten, Strength to encourage and sustain our rulers, and the Beauty of Holiness to adorn all their works."

Oddly enough, the cornerstone so solemnly laid that rainy day cannot be found today. Later granite-work surrounded and covered it completely.

While the Capitol project went on, Fuller's reputation traveled. The firm of Fuller & Laver was commissioned to design a City Hall in San Francisco—another monumental edifice with a high dome. This was begun in 1875 and took twenty years to complete. Fuller's partner, Augustus Laver, went to San Francisco to supervise that job, while Fuller carried on in Albany.

But there was thunder on the left for Thomas Fuller.

*Cupola of old Capitol surveyed the scene as foundations began
taking form. State Library was between it and camera.
Building at left is presumed to be a portion of Congress Hall.
Below: supporting pillars of Central Court arise in basement.*

The earliest granite blocks came out of an Adirondack quarry
north of Saratoga Springs. The handling of them was a constant
source of entertainment to townsmen, but spectators were warned
not to bother workmen. Below: first-story walls in progress.

The young gentleman at left is standing on what evidently was the cornerstone, the date of photo being September, 1871.
Note dividing line between Saratoga stone and white Maine granite.
Construction pictures by courtesy of State Architect's Office.

4. BATTLE OF THE STYLES

*Strata of disparate styles
are illustrated in a corner
tower of Capitol. At bottom
is seen first the Romanesque
balustrade, a Perry postscript.
Fuller's Italian Renaissance
speaks out in lower two stories:
typical are rough-hewn arches.
Third story was transitional.
Above its coping is belt-course
of incised arabesque work,
dividing line between styles.
Fourth story is pure Romanesque.
Then French Renaissance took over
as architect outwitted Legislature.*

Afterwards, someone asked Leopold Eidlitz "what business" he had to graft a Romanesque type of architecture upon Thomas Fuller's Italian Renaissance. "What business," Eidlitz countered, "had Fuller to put that basement under my building?"

The barbed witticism suggests the architectural crisis that arose when—after the Capitol was eight years along and going into its third story—a decision was taken to change architects in midstream. The immediate backfire was a hot debate that flared up in the profession, spread through the press, and was referred to as the "Battle of the Styles."

Clamor against the building had grown strident. Hostility to its ballooning cost spilled over into attacks on its design. More and more, it was being disparaged as a "white elephant." The $4,000,000 barrier was breached by 1874. The architect's estimate now was that it would require $8,000,000 more.

The Capitol was a scapegoat for political inquiries. The Senate Finance Committee, after an 1874 study, concluded that the system under which the work had been done was "not a wise one." The job ought to be "in the hands of one responsible man, who should be a practical builder, of large experience." Such a man was James W. Eaton, an Albany building contractor. Governor Dix named him superintendent of construction. Efficiency picked up, but the hue and cry did not subside.

31

Responsible persons felt that something besides the working system was radically wrong. What could it be unless the basic design?

Samuel J. Tilden, popular because of his fight to smash the Tweed Ring, was rewarded with the governorship in 1875. Along with him, as Lieutenant Governor, came William Dorsheimer, a Buffalo attorney with a good amateur knowledge of the fine arts. Reform being their watchword, it was to be anticipated that this team would "do something" about the new Capitol. What they did was in fact sensational.

The Capitol Commission had been boosted to eight members, none of whom knew much about construction. Governor Tilden began by ousting it and substituting a three-man ex officio Commission, made up of the Lieutenant Governor as chairman, the Attorney-General, and the auditor of the Canal Department. Thus Dorsheimer was handed a unique opportunity to work his will on the partly-finished building, and to leave behind a controversy that would linger down the decades.

Nobody had given the Fuller plan a genuinely critical examination since the work began. Dorsheimer did so, and thought there must be some better way in which to complete the building. So far, it was solid, but also stolid. It was evident that Fuller's mind had been mainly on the exterior, and that he had done little towards making the interior conform or giving it any refinement. For instance, he was going to seat the Assembly facing north, directly into the glare of the windows. The ceilings of both legislative chambers were to be undistinguished, of flat cast-iron.

The Dorsheimer commission approached its problem in much the way a family physician might treat a patient who was gravely ill: it called in some specialists for consultation. It engaged an Advisory Board of three members. Two of these were top-rank New York architects, Leopold Eidlitz and Henry H. Richardson. The third was the best-known landscape architect of his day, Frederick Law Olmsted, creator of Manhattan's Central Park. Olmsted fitted into the picture partly because he was a recognized arbiter of good taste in buildings and public works, partly because he was expected to do the landscaping once the Capitol was completed.

Quite possibly Dorsheimer planned in advance to have the "advisors" supplant Fuller. He already knew and admired Richardson; they were both Harvard men, and Richardson had designed a home for Dorsheimer in Buffalo. Moreover, the Commission asked them to supplement their report with diagrams of recommended changes. Obviously, this would have been done only if an alteration in style of architecture was in contemplation.

It was a somewhat embarrassing task that was handed these three men—to pick apart the work of a professional contemporary. The defects were not hard to find, but the cure was another thing. The only real cure, a perceptive writer remarked, would have been "the heroic remedy of dynamite." A newspaper diagnosed the case as follows: "The thing was thrown like a bone to competitors, and was snatched up and carried off by a sturdy builder innocent of any knowledge of the first principles of architecture, and backed by an army of greedy contractors. The sole aim of the design offered was to make a stunning show, to out-Herod Herod with tawdry magnificence on the outside and to let the comfort and convenience, nay the absolute necessities of the business of the legislators and judges for whose sole use the building was intended, go hang."

The report of the Advisory Board was delivered to the Senate in March of 1876. It was written by Olmsted, who had a way with a pen. At the outset, it said what could be said in favor of Fuller's design: "We know of no structure for civic purposes of modern times in which regard for stability and endurance is better evinced."

Leopold Eidlitz

These are the men who made over the Capitol—the Advisory Board. Eidlitz and Richardson, architects, divided building between them, interiorly, for working purposes. Eidlitz, with "fine Tennysonian face," was intellectual of the two, stout Richardson the sensualist. Former did the Assembly Chamber latter the Senate. Richardson introduced the Romanesque note. Olmsted, who was outstanding landscape architect of his day, worked out a landscaping plan for Capitol, never fully realized.

32

But the foundations were worthy of a better-conceived building, commensurate with "the grandeur of the Empire State."

This building, the Board said, simply lacked "repose and dignity." They enumerated what they considered its many flaws. The upper walls did not suggest the importance of the legislative chambers they were to contain, and ought to be "more elegantly formed, richer in detail." The roof had "too much outrigging and top hamper." They would accept the tower, but wished to modify its shape. By no possibility, they ruled, could the required accommodations of the Capitol "be conveniently arranged on the ground plan of the present building"—a plan that could not be rectified without starting over. The central open court was a prime stumbling-block. They bore down upon the location of the Senate and Assembly Chambers on the third floor ("as remote from the entrances as they could well be"), and this was another fault it was too late to correct. There was "waste space" everywhere. In place of an unimpressive flight of front steps planned by Fuller, they proposed a curious, semicircular "advanced terrace" formed of a series of vaulted arches, with a tesselated pavement on its roof. The reasoning behind this was that the Capitol stood on a slope, and that the jutting terrace would counteract the feeling that it was "in danger of sliding down the steep grade."

Sketches were attached indicating how the advisors would transform the upper stories and roof. The Capitol Commission adopted the recommendations promptly and informed the Senate, in a glow of optimism, that the building could now be finished for an additional $4,500,000 (except for the tower and approaches); and that it could be ready for occupancy, in toto, by January 1, 1879.

Thomas Fuller was dismissed as of July 1, 1876. He kept the office of Fuller & Laver in Albany five more years, while listing his home successively at Lake George and Burlington, Vermont. Then he returned to Ottawa and rounded out his life as Dominion architect of Canada. Death came to him in 1898, just as the final touches were being put on the Albany Capitol.

The three advisors who had pulled the rug out from under Fuller were appointed as joint architects of the Capitol. Though each maintained his separate business, they organized a firm to carry on the Albany work—Eidlitz, Richardson & Company. Olmsted was its treasurer.

Already the storm of controversy was raging, triggered by publication of the Eidlitz-Richardson sketches. These were printed in the March 11, 1876, issue of *The American Architect and Building News,* a Boston weekly that was the oracle of the architectural profession. Before long, its editor, W. P. P. Longfellow (a nephew of the poet) was writing: "We doubt if any occurrence in this generation has done more to weaken the general confidence in architects as architects . . . than this unlucky quarrel."

The pictures clearly showed a Romanesque style superimposed upon Italian Renaissance. To most conventionally trained architects, such a forced marriage of two distinct classes of architecture was rank heresy. Romanesque was earlier than Renaissance, having arisen out of the fall of the Roman Empire. When civilization bestirred itself again, it found the ruins of Roman structures scattered about western Europe. Awakening architects adopted the arches and vaults of the Roman engineers, but made a real art of these forms, and this was Romanesque. Gothic and Renaissance styles had superseded it, and Romanesque had been neglected for centuries. Then H. H. Richardson, thirsting for fresh inspiration, turned back to Romanesque, adding what came to be known as the "Richardsonian touch." And this is how Romanesque crept into the New York Capitol.

Richardson and Eidlitz felt they could make a transition between the two styles

Henry H. Richardson

Frederick Law Olmsted

that would not be too jarring, inasmuch as both types employed rounded arches (Gothic arches being pointed). They wondered, as Olmsted put it, if "the sap of one style can flow into the other." Inwardly distressed at the criticism of so many of their brother architects, these two always considered that what they did was not so much a question of clashing styles, as of taking a wholly bad building and making it partly good.

The tempest burst with formal remonstrances to the Legislature and outraged letters to newspapers and periodicals. The most stinging of these came from the New York Chapter of the American Institute of Architects (of which Richardson was a member). It was in the form of a remonstrance to the Senate, signed by the chapter president, Richard M. Hunt, himself an outstanding architect. "The chapter finds," said this diatribe, "that the projected work is designed in direct antagonism to the received rules of art. . . . [The] chapter most respectfully prays that you will not, by causing the construction of this design, establish a great public example which will stand for ages, in all its grandeur of proportion and magnificence of material, to vitiate public taste by its extreme incongruities of form and ornamentation." If the existing structure was so bad as all that, the chapter suggested, it might better be taken down and commenced anew.

Fuller spoke up in his own behalf with a communication to the Senate, rejecting the criticisms of the Advisory Board point by point, and insisting that the grafting of a different style "on a building so far advanced, would present a most unsightly appearance."

Governor Tilden held himself aloof from the seething argument. His only recorded comment on the new design was: "How much will it save?"

Despite all, no American architect ever before had such a glittering opportunity as was afforded Eidlitz and Richardson. With Lieutenant Governor Dorsheimer as their powerful champion, they were given virtual carte blanche. For a few years, the Capitol was their plaything. Dorsheimer's view was that the building should be "a school of architecture in itself to the people of the State." There is a hint, however, in a letter of Olmsted's, that the Lieutenant Governor kept some check-rein on their exuberance: "Dorsheimer, though yielding to professional judgment in the end, has from the first stood in the attitude of remonstrance and resistance to what he has designated as the 'over-sumptuous' inclinations both of Eidlitz and Richardson."

The two architects had not previously been associated. They were disparate characters, both strong individualists. Eidlitz, considerably the elder, was a devotee of Gothic, while Richardson was adventuring in Romanesque. And yet they hit it off admirably together. This was partly because they were wise enough to divide the interior of the Capitol between them. In a general way, Eidlitz took the Assembly side, Richardson the Senate side. Eidlitz did the Assembly Chamber, the Assembly and Senate staircases, the Golden Corridor, and the first Court of Appeals courtroom. Richardson did the Senate Chamber, the Executive Chamber, the Lieutenant Governor's office, the Great Western Staircase, and the second Court of Appeals courtroom. Each left the stamp of his personality indelibly upon the building.

Leopold Eidlitz, in his mid-fifties, was an immigrant of Jewish parentage, a native of Prague. He was a man of intense vitality and keen, flashing intellect, who kept abreast of the thought currents of his day. His ideal in architecture was "a scientific solution for an artistic problem." While Gothic was his chosen medium, he was no more content with slavish imitation than Richardson in his Romanesque. Eidlitz never could resist the Oriental touch: he loved to embroider his Gothic forms with Moorish-Saracenic ornament—hence the compari- *(Text continues on page 38)*

Lieut.-Governor Dorsheimer (top) was key figure in decision to revise Capitol architecture; also envisioned the building as a repository for fine arts. Building superintendent during controversy was James W. Eaton. Photo at left shows approximate stage at which Fuller left off, view from Washington Avenue side. Note, at right side of picture, projecting structure for balcony intended to flank Assembly Chamber. The new architects removed this; street-level portico was added later.

The evolution of a building: *The picture on page opposite is a
heliotype of Fuller's original design, as published
in* The American Architect *(1876). Presumably it was taken
from the scale model (cost, $4,000) exhibited on the grounds.
Above, the first sketch submitted by Advisory Board,
which triggered "Battle of the Styles." Below, later amendment
of that plan, showing the "advanced terrace" idea in front.*

(Text continues from page 35) son of some of his Capitol work to the Spanish Alhambra. He had designed P. T. Barnum's fabulous home, "Iranistan," at Bridgeport, Connecticut —a so-called Oriental villa, with minarets and spires, that combined Byzantine, Moorish, and Turkish architecture.

Richardson was the sybarite of the pair, an enormous man of large appetites, corpulent and yet not gross. Louisiana-born (in 1838), he went to Harvard, then to the École des Beaux Arts. The Civil War threw him into a quandary: his impulse was to return to his native South, but he decided, with much travail of soul, to remain in the North. He possessed "the build and driving force of a bison"—carried his great weight so actively that no one thought of him as being a fat man. He was a gourmet, a connoisseur of fine foods and wines, and lived with gusto—shrugging off the warnings of doctors (he was the victim of a chronic kidney disease). Similarly, he was fond of richness, warmth, and color in his architecture. A touring Dutch architect, upon being introduced to Richardson, exclaimed: "How you are like your buildings!"

Eidlitz, Richardson & Company went blithely ahead while the "Battle of the Styles" dinned in their ears. They began by taking down some courses of Fuller's stone-work above the coping of the second floor. Upon more mature thought, they had worked out modifications that made the transitional third story less jolting than it had seemed in the preliminary sketches. When the wall of this story was done, just above its coping and all the way around the building Eidlitz interposed a belt-course that is one of his typical Oriental gestures. It is a band of deeply incised arabesque work, and it says as plainly as words: From here on, this building was done by Eidlitz and Richardson.

While the architects made no public attempt to defend their alterations, they were by no means insensitive to the criticisms. Olmsted revealed their "annoyance and worry" in a brisk correspondence he carried on with Charles Eliot Norton, professor of the history of art at Harvard. Norton indicated his sympathy: "I can well understand what a difficult and ungrateful task you have had in trying to get this building into shape." Olmsted was obsessed with the subject, and poured out his feelings to the professor. Towards the end of that hectic year (1876), he calmed down enough to write:

"The design of the Capitol has since last winter grown more Romanesque but also, I hope, a little more quiet and coherent. There will be much historical incongruity in it and some that I would gladly have escaped. But we must take men as we find them and Eidlitz would not if he could have it otherwise. If he had been a man who could and would, we might have more weak and meaningless and pottering work, and it is a comfort that we are likely to escape that."

Not surprisingly, the big debate about architecture reverberated into the 1877 Legislature, and the upshot was another inquiry. The report strongly reflected the viewpoint of hostile architects: "The committee are of the opinion that it was not intended or expected by the Legislature creating the present commission that the style of architecture should be materially changed. . . . The Legislature desired to cheapen the cost of construction if the same was practicable, without lessening the beauty of the structure. . . . To employ two distinct styles of architecture of opposite principles and entirely different in character, on one and the same building or façade, is illogical and incongruous in the extreme, and admits of no defense. . . . Indeed, the folly of attempting to unite the two styles is revolting, not simply to trained professional taste, but to that common sense of harmony which belongs to every eye and mind."

The committee, after expounding at length on the theory of architecture, got around to recommending "that the exterior of the New Capitol be completed in the

Richard M. Hunt signed remonstrance to Senate against change in style. A fashionable architect of the day, he was brother of William M. Hunt who did Assembly Chamber murals. Right, a study in diverse styles: The wall is Italian Renaissance, rugged and fortress-like; deep cut horizontal lines are rustication, a typical aspect of that style. The arch itself is Romanesque. Beyond is Albany City Hall tower, erected by Richardson at period when he was working on the Capitol, a fine example of his Romanesque.

The Great Gable, of west façade, is lushest item of exterior. Loggia is the central feature. Between its arches are Roman deities, Justitia and Puritas. In lower angles of tympanum are winged Babylonian lions. Massive finial is remarkable. Directly beneath the loggia are symbolic American eagles. Smaller photos draw contrast between dormers: the one above is Richardsonian Renaissance; below, an Eidlitz dormer done for the open central court.

Renaissance style and in conformity with the original design on which it has thus far been erected."

Two members of the five-man committee dissented in a minority report; insisted that the Commission, by making the change, had in fact "rendered the State service of great value in overcoming glaring defects of portions of the old plan."

Now there happened an astonishing thing, perhaps unparalleled in history. The Legislature of the State of New York actually legislated architecture. In making the 1877 appropriation to continue the work, the Legislature attached a rider directing the Commission to "build and complete the exterior of the New Capitol building in the Italian Renaissance style of architecture adopted in the original design, and according to the style upon which the building was being erected prior to the adoption of the so-called 'modified design'."

Eidlitz and Richardson must have been greatly taken aback—but they managed in a subtle way to have the last laugh. There exists a letter which Richardson wrote to their partner, Olmsted, at this juncture, containing the sly remark:

"I do believe entre nous that the building can be well finished in Francois 1st or Louis XIV, which come under the head of Renaissance."

But *not* under the head of Italian Renaissance. Richardson changed signals and designed the roof features in French Renaissance with a decidedly "Richardsonian" flavor. It does not appear that the legislators ever recognized the difference.

Another storm was brewing.

When Governor Tilden ran for the presidency in 1876, his personal choice for a successor at Albany was Lieutenant Governor Dorsheimer. Had Dorsheimer become Governor, the Capitol, in all likelihood, would have moved along to speedier and happier culmination. But the Democratic convention, while retaining Dorsheimer as Lieutenant Governor, nominated Lucius Robinson of Elmira for the governorship. The fact that Dorsheimer openly opposed Robinson's nomination did nothing to sweeten the relationship between these two unlike men after they won the election.

Lucius Robinson was a tight-lipped, economy-minded man. They said of him that he had figured out the interest on the cost of the Capitol to date and announced that it would keep Chemung County in a permanent supply of chewing-tobacco.

This new Governor declared overt war on the Capitol. When the 1877 Legislature passed an appropriation of $1,000,000 to continue it, he vetoed the bill. The veto message was a tirade: "The New Capitol is a great public calamity. . . . It is without a parallel for extravagance and folly. . . . It is more than double the size needed for a Capitol. . . . When this great and useless structure can or will be completed it is idle to conjecture . . ."

The Legislature cut the appropriation to $500,000 and passed it by a vote large enough to repass it over a veto if need be. The Governor let it stand. But he did not cease, as long as he was in office, to fulminate against the "public calamity."

The lesser appropriation compelled the Commission to lower its sights. It was manifestly impossible to complete the building by January 1, 1879. All right, then, they would complete a piece of it. A decision was taken to apply all available funds to finishing up the "North Center" in time for occupancy on that date. The "North Center" was the section to contain the Assembly Chamber.

As the work went along, the allied architects would make their trips to Albany on the Hudson River night-boat. Usually they were accompanied by Olmsted, and sometimes by Lieutenant Governor Dorsheimer. Eidlitz would have a roll of working drawings under his arm, not trusting them out of his sight. Where this little group settled on deck, there the conversation sparkled while moonlight danced on the river. A sculptor who once accompanied them recalled: "There was never so much wit and humor and science and art on that boat before or since."

5. HOUSE-WARMING

There was no heat in the Assembly Chamber of the old Capitol that cold winter's morning. It was not going to be used, ever again. In fact, the chamber already was stripped of its desks and carpets.

As a matter of form, however, the members of Assembly came together in the cheerless room on January 7, 1879, merely to take their farewell of it. They kept their overcoats on, against the chill, and stood about nervously waiting for the Senate, which was upstairs having a caucus.

After 20 minutes, the worn stairs creaked. The Senators came down by pairs, led by Lieutenant Governor Dorsheimer and the Attorney General, Augustus Schoonmaker, Jr. As the line passed the Assembly door, the members fell in behind. The procession filed out between the Ionic pillars, down the familiar tree-lined walk for the last time, and tramped through the snow from the old Capitol to the completed portion of the new one.

Washington Avenue was alive with spectators, for this was a big day for Albany.

At the entrance of the "North Center" the legislators were welcomed by James W. Eaton, the building superintendent. He guided them up the Assembly Staircase and into the wondrous Assembly Chamber. It was the first glimpse most of them had of this room, the fame of which already was nation-wide—"the grandest legislative hall in the world."

The Assembly Chamber when new, as sketched by Harper's artist, with sight-seers admiring it. He used his imagination somewhat, as he left out seats and desks. Members had moved in before the public was allowed to see. In vista through magnificent groined arches may be viewed one of the famed Hunt murals.

Lieutenant Governor Dorsheimer—and certainly there was a thrill of pride in his own bosom at this moment—mounted the rostrum, banged the gavel, and intoned:

"The Senate has escorted the Assembly from the old Capitol to the new one. And now, in this presence, I declare the chambers formally transferred to the Legislature. The Senate will now retire to its own room."

Strictly speaking, the Senate did not yet have a room of its own. The Senate Chamber would not be ready for another two years. In the meantime, the Senate would sit in the oak-panelled courtroom built for the Court of Appeals. This was on the floor below the Assembly, and it opened upon the Golden Corridor. (A quip was heard about the Senate's having become the "Lower House.")

The temporary chambers of the Governor, also off the Golden Corridor, were to the east of the temporary Senate Chamber. A rumor was going the rounds that Governor Robinson did not intend to recognize the existence of the new Capitol and would refuse to deliver his annual message inside its walls. A newspaper report said: "It has been stated that the Governor objects to occupying his new quarters at present, but it is certainly difficult to perceive why he does so, or concede the soundness of his reasons for remaining in his present cramped, uncomfortable and ill-ventilated quarters."

Lucius Robinson did not have much difficulty in resembling a sphinx, and that is how he looked when reporters questioned him about his intentions.

Neither house stayed in session more than an hour that Tuesday. A "snow blockade" had crippled railroad traffic from the west so that many legislators had been unable to reach Albany. Besides that, who could get down to business when the "North Center" was being festively opened? The town was teeming with important visitors, and the Capitol would be the scene of a lavish reception that evening.

The Senate had intended to play host for this reception. Just before adjourning the previous session, each Senator had donated $50 to that end. But the citizens of Albany had snatched the ball away from the Senate, deciding it would be more appropriate for them to sponsor the opening. A Society of the Capital was formed and donations solicited. Each $25 subscriber got a ticket of admission for the reception. Invitations went out to 4,000 persons of note throughout the state.

The committee made the gesture of asking Governor Robinson to do the receiving. Not unexpectedly, he refused. Another invitation related to the event was rebuffed by the Governor. The Albany Burgesses Corps, a fashionable drill corps, planned a New Capitol Ball in a downtown hall. Officers of the Burgesses Corps tactfully announced that the Governor had declined to attend the ball "for reasons which he frankly gave that quite forbid it."

The attitude of the Governor explains why, that evening, the official "receiving" in the gubernatorial office of the new Capitol was performed by the Mayor of Albany, Michael Nolan, as chairman of the citizens' committee. Lieutenant Governor Dorsheimer hovered over the affair in general, mingling with the guests, relishing the plaudits.

Not merely the local press described the evening as "the most brilliant social event in the history of Albany." An endless parade of sleighs moved down Washington Avenue to discharge passengers at the only entrance yet available. Ladies in dazzling gowns, decked with jewels, alighted on the arms of distinguished escorts. Full-dress predominated. An estimated 10,000 people came and went.

With only an approximate one-fourth of the building open, such a number meant a human traffic jam. Everyone took the grand tour: up the Assembly Staircase, through the Golden Corridor with a detour into the Court of Appeals (Senate Chamber, pro tem), and on up to the pièce de resistance, the Assembly Chamber. The stately stairway was a solid stream of humanity, half of it struggling upward meeting the other half coming back. To be sure, there were elevators (steam lifts): these were described as "elaborate and beautiful apartments in themselves," finished in carved hardwood.

Part of the plan had been to have dancing in the Golden Corridor, but the crush was so great that it had to be given up. Two name-bands of the era were playing, however—one in the Golden Corridor, the other on the floor of the Assembly Chamber. They played music like the Quartette from "Rigoletto," Weber's "Invitation to the Dance," Rossini's Overture to "Semiramide," and Strauss waltzes.

It was as much an architectural as a social occasion. Seldom has an American architect had so triumphant an hour as did Leopold Eidlitz. The interior, at least, of the "North Center" was completely his. Eidlitz stood in the Assembly Chamber, a radiant look on his "fine Tennysonian face." The praises of his work rang in his ears. John Hay, who had been Lincoln's secretary, stood near him, gazing at the incredible

Governor Lucius Robinson (above) hated the new Capitol so much he would not occupy his Chamber. The Golden Corridor, at right, is a good sample of his reasons. This wondrous passage glowed with color patterns to excel palace of an Oriental potentate. Visitors were as much dazzled as by Assembly Chamber itself. Windows bordered on Central Cour Unhappily, the structure cracked and Golden Corridor was doomed. A row of offices supplanted it.

ceiling, and exclaimed: "What a great thing to have done in this country!"

Eagle-eyed reporters looked around and saw celebrities like Edward Everett Hale and George W. Curtis; General Dan Sickles, who had left a leg at Gettysburg; David Dudley Field, the noted attorney; a couple of ex-Governors, Horatio Seymour and John T. Hoffman. Special homage was paid to the venerable Thurlow Weed, erstwhile "Dictator" of the Whig Party, at 81 the oldest former legislator on the scene.

Eidlitz had done a spectacularly daring thing with the ceiling of his Assembly Chamber. He had given it the most wide-spanning groined stone arch ever attempted in the annals of architecture. The keystone of the central vault (weight, three tons) was 56 feet above the floor. While the chamber was emphatically Gothic in style, it was strongly marked with Eidlitz' penchant for the Oriental. The ribs and groins of the stone arches were embroidered with incised decoration, colored with vermilion and ultramarine and edged with gold. Upholding the arches were four huge pillars of polished red granite. In the high lunettes of the north and south walls were the allegorical murals just finished by William Morris Hunt. Rows of stained-glass windows were below the murals. The stone walls were carved in intaglio figures, the ground of which was colored vermilion. There were two wonderfully carved stone fireplaces under the galleries, and a blank stone frieze around the walls which was intended to be carved with historical bas-reliefs by a noted sculptor (it never was).

The Golden Corridor was scarcely less adorned than the Assembly Chamber. More than anything else in the Capitol, this hall deserved the term "Alhambresque," and it is one of the vanished splendors. On the second floor, it was lighted by the windows of the Central Court. It was 140 feet long, 25 feet wide, 27 feet high, and its "mass of gorgeous color" excited gasps of admiration. The ceiling, on a smaller scale, was somewhat similar to that of the Assembly Chamber, a series of groined stone arches. This ceiling was a diaper of blue, red and umber on a ground of gold. The Golden Corridor lasted little more than a decade.

Only in the Assembly Staircase did Eidlitz resist his inclination for the Moorish type of decoration. This pioneer of the Capitol's stairways is straight Victorian Gothic, in the English sense—a mounting series of graceful, pointed arches in a square well that was then topped by a skylight.

Eidlitz also had taken as part of his task the finishing of the Grand Central Court bequeathed them by Fuller. He treated it with dormers that are distinctly different from Richardson's dormers on the exterior walls. They have bands of arabesque carving, and also carry the finely carved coats-of-arms of various prominent early American families.

Despite wintry weather, the roofless inner court that night of the reception was utilized for a refreshment tent. Mounds of food were supplied by caterers. Those who patronized it found a "cool lunch-room," even though heat was piped into the tent.

Around 10 o'clock, a whisper ran through the jostling throng. The Governor was coming, after all.

Reluctantly, Governor Robinson had decided it wouldn't do for him to ignore such an occasion altogether. He strode through, escorted by his staff with cocked hats and swords. The visitation lasted but 20 minutes. A reporter pictured the Governor as seeming to be "annoyed with the scene" and "not deigning to look a pleasure he did not feel."

The public house-warming was well and good, and legislators attended it. But it did not cover all the initiation which the law-makers felt to be the just due of the new Capitol. Therefore, the Legislature scheduled a formal ceremony of its own for the

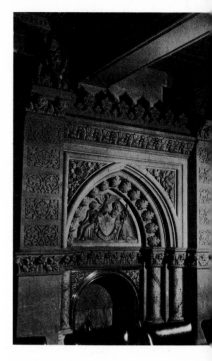

Elaborate fireplaces abound.
Pictured above is one of pair
Eidlitz gave Assembly Chamber.
At right is segment of
wall over Assembly entrance door,
with Saracenic intaglio carving
suggestive of the Alhambra.
Below: the Assembly rostrum,
with F. D. Roosevelt speaking,
Herbert Lehman seated beside.

evening of February 12, to take place in the Assembly Chamber. Of course, the Governor was invited.

Just as the program was about to begin, Lieutenant Governor Dorsheimer cleared his throat and read a communication from Governor Robinson, which said:

"I find, with extreme regret, that I shall be deprived of the privilege of listening to the addresses of yourself, Speaker Alvord and Mr. Brooks, this evening as I had hoped to do. Every moment of my time is occupied with official duties of unusual urgency. I see, moreover, by the morning papers, that the ceremonies are expected to occupy three or four hours, and I am advised by my oculist that there would be a great danger of entirely arresting the improvement going on with my eyes if I should expose them to the gas-lights in the Assembly Chamber even for one-fourth of that time, and he protests against it most earnestly."

A handsome big armchair had been provided for the Governor to sit in. It stood conspicuously vacant while speeches were made by Speaker Thomas G. Alvord, Assemblyman Erastus Brooks, and Lieutenant Governor Dorsheimer. The latter concluded by saying:

"When our future shall be the past, it must be that those who shall live then will rejoice that the Capitol has been built so strong that its associations and its traditions will endure to the latest generation."

As had been predicted, Governor Robinson obdurately refused to move his office from the old Capitol. When it came time to deliver his message to the Legislature, he sent his secretary over with it. The message was heavy with sarcasm where it touched upon the building:

"The event which first claims attention is your removal into the New Capitol. . . . I sincerely hope that you will find the change conducive to your health and comfort, and in every way so agreeable and convenient that you will not regret it. If the occupation of their new and gorgeous apartments shall lead the two houses of the Legislature to so emulate the exalted virtues which have, at different times and on many occasions, adorned the history of the old chambers, that they shall enact only wise and good laws; that they shall honestly and faithfully execute the great trust committed to them by the people; that they shall strictly obey the Constitution and the laws; that they shall establish and maintain a higher tone of public morality, the enormous cost of the building will be repaid in something better than money. But if, on the other hand, no such effects appear; if the lamentable vices, which have too often marked the legislation of the old building, shall stain that of the new; if the extravagant expenditure made upon it is to stimulate profuse and wasteful appropriations to other objects; if, instead of encouraging a plain and honest republican simplicity, it is to cultivate a weak and vain desire to imitate the manners of European courts or to rival regal magnificence and imperial splendours; nay, more, if bribery and corruption, following naturally in the wake of such influences, shall soil the new chambers, the people will have cause to regret the erection of such a Capitol, and to wish that the earth might open and swallow it up."

That autumn, a Tammany split in the Democratic party defeated Robinson for reelection. A Republican, Alonzo B. Cornell, succeeded him.

Governor Robinson restrained his antipathy to the building sufficiently to perform the traditional courtesy of escorting the incoming Governor to his inauguration. But his subconscious rejection of it evidently remained. Observers noted that he looked pale and ill as he entered the Assembly Chamber, arm in arm with Mr. Cornell.

In walking down the few steps to the floor of the Assembly, Governor Robinson tripped. He would almost certainly have fallen headlong had not the robust Governor-elect seized him firmly by the arm, helping him to regain balance.

*The Assembly Chamber—then and now. Picture at left
is obviously much "doctored." Suspicion persists
that many of faces of the legislators were glued in.
It is noticeable that each one is turned toward camera,
no matter how awkwardly. Hunt mural in upper corner.
The pictorial frieze between windows is outright hoax.
The frieze was intended to bear a series of historical
bas-reliefs by J. Q. A. Ward, but still remains blank.
Granite pillars today hint of grand ceiling of yore.*

The Assembly Staircase (right) was first
of the four grand stairways. It is purely
Victorian Gothic, designed by Eidlitz.
Incongruous round-arched windows in wall
were a later addition by Isaac Perry
when he knocked holes to let in the air.
Above: a couple stroll under visitors'
gallery of Assembly Chamber in 1880's.
Gas fixtures soon gave way to electricity.

The Senate had to be content with temporary
home for first two years in new Capitol.
This was it: the original Court of Appeals
chamber, next floor below the Assembly.
The judges later rejected the chamber
as inadequate, were placated with new one.
Segment of this room beyond the pillars
was walled off, in time, into a corridor,
the rest becoming the Court of Claims.

6. THE VANISHING MURALS

On dizzy scaffoldings 40 feet above the floor of the Assembly Chamber, a frail-looking man with the graying beard of a patriarch wielded brushes almost frantically during the autumn of 1878. Time pressed upon him, and his strength was hardly adequate to the task, though he did have the help of an assistant. He was applying oil pigments directly to the bare sandstone walls in the lunettes above the tall rows of stained-glass windows.

The man exulted in the work, and said: "I would rather carry out this project than be Governor of the state." To a friend he wrote: "I can tell you it is like sailing a 'seventy-four,' or riding eight horses in a circus. It fills one's lungs to breathe in front of such spaces."

Murals done by William M. Hunt embellished Assembly Chamber. "The Flight of Night," on north wall, depicted moon-goddess chasing darkness from sky; was brilliant and fiery. "The Discoverer" was symbolic of Columbus challenging ocean, Hope at prow, Fortune at tiller. It was virile in composition.

At this point the career of William Morris Hunt, aged 54, a studio painter and art-teacher of Boston, reached flood-tide. He had yearned to paint on a grand scale, and to escape the brahmin atmosphere of Boston in which he felt stifled. Hunt was a brother of Richard M. Hunt, a leading architect who had worked on the U. S. Capitol; and who, by coincidence, had signed the remonstrance against changing the style of the Albany Capitol. From study in Paris, the artist was an apostle of Couture and Millet. His easel work had merit, and Celia Thaxter, the poet, said of him: "Ah, he has the immortal spark if ever mortal had it!"

Release from the Boston conservatism he so deplored seemed to beckon in a letter Hunt received in June, 1878, from Leopold Eidlitz:

"It is proposed to have some allegorical or legendary paintings in the Assembly Chamber of the new Capitol at Albany. Lieutenant-Governor Dorsheimer thinks that you would be willing to give us some advice,—perhaps personal assistance in the matter; and requests that you call at my office to examine a sketch indicating the work to be done, with a view to a proposed engagement."

Hunt went to see Eidlitz, and they took an instant liking to each other. The architect sized Hunt up as "not only an artist, but a philosopher." He was engaged to paint two murals at a fee of $15,000, and was told the Chamber would be in shape for him to start by September—but that they must, at all costs, be finished in time for the January opening of the "North Center."

At that moment, the climate of the Capitol was remarkably favorable to the arts. Dorsheimer envisioned the building as not just a seat of government but a shrine of art. Fine paintings should adorn its walls and sculpture should inhabit its corridors. Hunt found himself instantly at home, and said: "Here I am in my own world, and I want to stay here." In fact, he was virtually promised a continuing contract for future painting in the Capitol, and began shaping plans to move to Albany permanently.

In his Boston studio, Hunt went immediately to work on charcoal cartoons for the murals. He was happy that the state wanted allegorical subjects, rather than historical. Two themes had been haunting his mind for years, and he already had done sketches on both. They were the complementary ideas of discovery and enlightenment: the one personified by Columbus, the other by the Persian moon-goddess, Anahita, driving darkness from the sky. Both themes begged for large treatment, and here was his chance. The space allowed him in each lunette was about 40 by 16 feet.

Hunt had invented a set of pigments which would dry unusually hard and with a luminous appearance. He ordered samples of the sandstone in the Chamber sent to him, and experimented with the pigments on the absorbent stone. The rest of his problem was the location of the murals—very high in the room and poorly lighted. To overcome this, he must use strong primary colors and heavy outlines.

Mural painting was an infant art in America at the time, and success with these paintings could open a whole new career for Hunt. The only comparable work as yet in existence was the frescoes of Constantino Brumidi in the national Capitol. What Hunt had to do was quite different. Frescoes are painted on wet plaster. Hunt was to paint on naked stone.

September came, and Hunt was told that the staging could not be ready for him until mid-October. This shortened by so much the time for a job that few artists would have wished to tackle with less than a year. When he could finally get at it, Hunt began by casting magic-lantern slides of his cartoons on the walls and tracing them to the proper size. The murals were begun on October 29 and finished on December 21.

He placed "The Discoverer" on the south wall, "The Flight of Night" on the north. Facing across the great Chamber at one another, the ideas were in philosophical counterpoint. They symbolized "the great opposing Forces which control all nature . . . Negative and Positive, Night and Day, Feminine and Masculine, Darkness and Light, Superstition and Science, Pagan and Divine Thought, Self and Altruism."

While he was painting them, he was enthralled by the bustle of the workmen down below, and began to think of future murals which would illustrate their labor —immortalizing them upon the walls of the very building they were erecting. Nothing pleased him more than when a bricklayer or hod-carrier climbed the ladder to make favorable comments on his work. "What a big thing a great building is," he wrote. "People grumble and whine about the money which is thrown away upon it; but I tell you that it is an immense work, and worthy of any state or nation. It is the greatest thing which this State has ever done, and a very sensible way to spend money."

Hunt passed much of his time in the studio of Erastus Dow Palmer, which was almost in the shadow of the rising Capitol. Palmer, a sculptor of national note, shared

Dorsheimer's dream of making the Capitol a repository of fine art.

Palmer had recently done a vigorous statue of Chancellor Robert R. Livingston for the Hall of Statuary in the U. S. Capitol. At his own expense, he made a second cast of it, in the hope that it could be placed in the New York Capitol. With Dorsheimer's help, he finally got the statue into the Golden Corridor, later into the Court of Appeals courtroom. But the State never purchased it, keeping it as a loan, and it finally came to rest in the rear of the present Court of Appeals.

Another hopeful sculptor during this period was J. Q. A. Ward, who was to do a series of historical bas-reliefs for the vacant frieze on the walls of the Assembly Chamber. The tightening of appropriations, however, cancelled this project. There was some posthumous justice for Ward in the fact that his model for an equestrian statue of General Philip Sheridan, with some finishing touches by Daniel Chester French, was adopted many years later for the Sheridan statue which today adorns Capitol Park.

Still another sculptural project which died a-borning was the bas-relief carving of the fireplace breasts in the Senate Chamber. Augustus Saint-Gaudens was all but signed up for this work when fiscal austerity forced cancellation of the work.

At any rate, William Morris Hunt finished his murals, and they stirred almost as much comment as the Chamber itself. Said one art critic: "Nothing as yet undertaken here in the art of monumental decoration at all approaches these mural paintings of Mr. Hunt, in the dignity of the composition as a whole, in the beauty of the parts, in the mastery of the execution." Though thoroughly exhausted from laboring under such pressure, Hunt was in the Chamber the night of the opening reception, "making an unsuccessful attempt to blush unseen."

Hunt's hopes for remaining permanently as a Capitol artist were soon dashed. Governor Robinson took an especially dim view of costly murals. The Legislature went along with him to the extent of cutting the 1879 appropriation in half and restricting the use of the money to the outside walls and the roof, "without any internal ornamentation."

After living in the clouds for a few short months, Hunt returned to Boston weakened and extremely depressed. That summer he accepted the invitation of Celia Thaxter and her husband to recuperate in a cottage at their summer estate in the Isles of Shoals. Soon after his arrival, Mrs. Thaxter wrote a friend: "Just think of our having William Hunt here, just shuddered back from the dreadful verge, so attenuated, so pathetic! . . . But he really is coming back to life, and eats and sleeps again."

One rainy morning in September, Hunt came into the Thaxters' house after breakfast and sat for a while chatting before the fire. The rain relenting, he got up and went out for a walk. When he did not reappear for two hours, his friends became alarmed. Mrs. Thaxter herself found his body floating in a small reservoir, facedown. The papers treated it as a case of suicide "caused by hypochondria, induced by close application."

The murals survived their painter by a scant 10 years.

The roof gutters of the "North Center" were made entirely of stone, without metal linings. They began to leak. Water seeped inside the walls and discolored the murals. Patches of paint flaked off.

Then the famous arched ceiling cracked dangerously. The flat wooden ceiling that replaced it, at a level twenty feet lower, sealed the paintings off altogether from public view. The upper portion of the figures, however, remained above the ceiling in the attic loft from which the Assembly lights and ventilation are operated. There, fragments of "The Discoverer" and "The Flight of Night" may still be seen—by Capitol maintenance men.

William Morris Hunt's last effort was the self-portrait at left, and mirrors his despondency. In Albany, he passed much time in nearby studio of the sculptor, Erastus Dow Palmer, who is seen below at work, with an understudy. Palmer likewise wished to make Capitol a repository of art, was in league with Dorsheimer. His sole contribution was statue of Chancellor Robert Livingston.

Hunt's murals were sentenced
to oblivion by new ceiling,
but stubborn fragments remain
in loft space above Chamber.
Despite time and moisture,
framed by ventilating ducts and
steam pipes, here is what
survives of "The Discoverer."
The heavy outlines the artist
found needful to make murals
stand out in their position
so far above floor are manifest.
Below: Harper's sketch shows
how mural looked in place.

Hall of Governors is corridor leading
to Executive Chamber, its walls lined by
oil portraits of past Governors.
E. D. Palmer's statue of Livingston,
now in Court of Appeals, is at left.
Above it, his original cast of State Seal,
enshrined at top of Western Staircase.
At right: statue of Gen. Philip Sheridan,
astride Rienzi, stands in Capitol Park.
Created from a model by J. Q. A. Ward,
to whom Sheridan had said "Be sure
and give me a horse," it was enlarged
by Daniel Chester French, unveiled in 1916.
Governor Martin Glynn crusaded for it.

The Red Room boasts its own art gallery,
of which these paintings are specimens.
Governor Charles Evans Hughes (right) posed
for Baltimore artist Thomas C. Corner.
Theodore Roosevelt (below) had his portrait
done by Ritter von Krumhaar, Washington.
Legislature commissioned the other two:
that of Lafayette (below right)
is fabulous in value, painted from life
during his last visit to America, in 1825,
by Charles Ingham; full-length study of
George Clinton, (opposite page)
state's first Governor, is by Ezra Ames.

7. BEAUTY FOR THE SENATE

The Senate Chamber soon won renown as America's most beautiful room. It has been the least changed of any major room in Capitol. Celebrated Mexican onyx panels cross middle of wall on left. Richardson's splendid case clock still does duty in far corner. Senate does not permit photos during session; this was informal.

While the Assembly was getting used to its dramatic new chamber, things began to happen on the Senate side, or "South Center." Now it was H. H. Richardson's turn to make frozen music.

Governor Cornell—son of the founder of Cornell University—was as frugal-minded as Lucius Robinson, but a shade more flexible. His view was that the Capitol was "so far advanced that there seems to be no rational course left but to provide for its completion in the most advantageous manner possible."

The 1880 Legislature loosened the purse-strings to the extent of $1,600,000, with the proviso that "the Senate chamber shall be completed and furnished and ready for occupation by the Senate on the 1st day of January, 1881."

Another deadline for an architect to meet. Richardson had more leeway, however, than had been vouchsafed to Eidlitz on the Assembly side. His plans for both the Senate and Executive Chambers were well in hand long before there was any roof over the South Center.

In some of the design detail of the Senate Chamber, Richardson had the services of a promising young man who had been an understudy in his office. This disciple was Stanford White, who would make his own mark as an architect before being unfortunately shot to death by Harry K. Thaw.

In May, 1878, White confided in his sculptor friend, Saint-Gaudens, that he and Richardson had "just tackled the Albany Senate Chamber, and between us cooked up something pretty decent." Doubtless it was Stanford White who suggested having Saint-Gaudens do the sculptures for the Senate fireplaces—an idea which never materialized.

Although the Capitol's best friend, Lieutenant Governor Dorsheimer, went out of office at just about this time (he later became Federal District Attorney for Southern New York), his influence lingered long enough for Richardson to make his suave and elegant contributions to the interior. The architect was able to lavish such sensitivity and loving care upon the Senate Chamber that it would be hailed as the "most beautiful room in the United States." By this time, Richardson had moved his offices from New York to Boston.

Even while the Senate Chamber was taking shape, its creator was drawn into the worries of his partner, Eidlitz, about the Assembly Chamber. The bad omens began almost as soon as it was occupied. The acoustics were atrocious. The magnificent ceiling was visually good but aurally hopeless. It swallowed sound and tossed echoes. The acoustical defects caused blunders in legislation. An Assemblyman voted against his own bill—by mistake. Some bills got so muddled in this way that they were recalled from the Governor to save them from veto.

After shouting itself hoarse, the Assembly took the usual measure: it appointed a committee. The committee took it up with the architects. The architects denied there was any "organic acoustic defect," and blamed the trouble on the freedom of visitors to ramble about the room during session and "indulge in conversation." They suggested raising the Speaker's desk a few inches and moving the seats of members closer together. This was no improvement.

There was another, more ominous thing. Barely a month before the 1880 Legislature was due to convene, Superintendent Eaton spotted a crack in a stone of the ceiling. Eidlitz came hurrying up from New York. The stone was replaced. Eidlitz juggled equations to reassure himself that the lines of stress in his arches were all right. Two engineers were hired to make a study. They reported that some uneven settling may have occurred in the foundations, but that it was safe for the Assembly to occupy its chamber.

The Assembly met, albeit with some uneasy glances at the ceiling. No more cracks were in sight. But then the members heard that chinks were appearing in the abutments of the Golden Corridor, right under them. The whole Assembly took a walk downstairs to see, and found the report true. After all, such a weighty building did have a lot of settling to do....

Richardson, meanwhile, was composing a symphony of a room. The Senate Chamber is generally regarded as the handsomest room he ever did. Moreover, it was so well built and decorated that it has since undergone fewer changes than any major room in the Capitol.

Richardson had the same box-like space as Eidlitz with which to contend. Yet he needed much less space to accommodate a legislative body of only thirty-two members. There was little he could do about its height, but he could pull in the walls. This he did by treating both ends as lobbies, placing the visitors' galleries above them.

Mindful of Eidlitz' acoustical troubles with the Assembly Chamber, he tried nothing adventurous with the Senate ceiling. He left it flat, though of richly carved and deep-panelled oak.

One can almost imagine Richardson fondling this room. He had an uncanny feeling for the qualities, tones, and textures of building materials, and employed them almost as a painter might his pigments. He brought onyx from Mexico, Siena marble from Italy, red granite from Scotland. The Mexican onyx panelling of the north and south walls always has been one of the famous features of this exquisite chamber. The ultimate in luxury was attained with red leather and carved mahogany panelling on the walls below the galleries.

For a while, the Capitol maintained the equivalent of a furniture factory within its own walls. No commonplace commercial furniture for such architects as these! Richardson and Eidlitz designed the furniture for their rooms. Several of Richardson's Senate chairs, including his original Lieutenant Governor's chair, may still be seen in the corridors. He also designed a few superb tall case clocks, one of which is

The presence on the rostrum of Senator Dennis McCarthy seemingly pinpoints 1885 as the year of this scene. He was president of Senate for that session. It is another tinkered picture, in which heads obviously have been dubbed in. One of the unadorned fireplace breasts is seen at right; these were to have been sculptured by Saint-Gaudens.

still the official Senate timepiece, while another stands sedately in the Senate corridor.

While Richardson was working on the Senate Chamber, the City Hall of Albany burned. His involvement with the Capitol led to his engagement to design a new City Hall, which he did in Romanesque style and completed in 1881.

Owing to lay-offs of laborers and sundry other difficulties, the Senate Chamber did not quite meet its deadline. The Senate occupied it on March 10, 1881, and it still required some finishing touches.

On the opening of the new chamber, the Assembly returned the courtesy of two years before. It escorted the Senate across the building for a formal ceremony. The galleries were jammed, mainly by the fair sex. Lieutenant Governor George G. Hoskins presided, and boasted of the room that "for permanence, beauty and pleasing effect, I believe its superior cannot be found on this continent, or even in the wide world."

Assemblyman James W. Husted of Peekskill was inspired to poetical quotation, and said that the room reminded him of a line from Keats: "A thing of beauty is a joy forever."

Richardson finished the Executive Chamber at approximately the same time as the Senate Chamber, Governor Cornell being the first to occupy it. The architect's passion for warm color and luxury also went into this spacious room (60 by 40 feet). He treated its walls with a high wainscot of panelled mahogany, and above this with Spanish leather. The handsome beams of a carved-oak ceiling topped it off. Of several spectacular fireplaces in the Capitol, that in the Executive Chamber is one of the best. Governors for a long time actually used this chamber as an office. In late years, they have sought the privacy of a smaller adjoining office, and the "Red Room"—as it is called nowadays—is open to the public, and is used by Governors only for hearings and ceremonial occasions.

Richardson likewise designed the Lieutenant Governor's office, close to the Senate Chamber—a perfect gem of a room which, however, is purely a working office and is rarely seen by the public.

When the Senate moved into its own Chamber, the Court of Appeals courtroom which it had been occupying was released for its original purpose. For some obscure reason the judges did not like it. Governor Cornell told the 1882 Legislature:

"The Judges of the Court of Appeals express dissatisfaction with the apartments designed for their use, and seem unwilling to occupy them at present. They desire to have rooms set apart for them in another quarter of the building, and have indicated a preference for a portion of the space originally intended for the State Library."

Because the high court judges were so hard to please, another superb Richardson room was added to the Capitol. The substitute courtroom was placed in the southeast corner of the third floor, directly above the Executive Chamber. With this the judiciary was satisfied. (The room was moved intact in 1917 to its present location in the Court of Appeals Building.)

Amid the architectural juggling, the State Library—originally planned to extend across the front of the building on the third and fourth floors—was shifted to the same relative position on the west side.

H. H. Richardson died in April, 1886, at the age of forty-eight. He would not heed the doctors. Aesthete he was, but ascetic he would not be.

William Dorsheimer, the former Lieutenant Governor who had lured him to Albany, paid him this tribute:

"There is no painter or sculptor, nor, as we think, any living poet, who has won a reputation so enduring. . . . No one used architectural forms with so much originality, no one with so much grace and tenderness, no one with such strength; nor has any one ever so impressed them with his own personal individuality."

A few Richardson masterpieces. Above: one of the fine case clocks stands in Senate Corridor. The Lieutenant Governor's office (right) is a room little known to the public, but a perfect gem; Richardson clock stands on mantel. Below: Lieutenant Governor's original chair, now a showpiece. Far right: architect's own sketch of clock for Court of Appeals.

Executive Chamber is another memorable Richardson room.
Governor Rockefeller is seen at desk signing a bill.
In latter times, Governors occupy a smaller private office.
Mahogany wainscot surrounds chamber, while the upper wall
has a modern stencil design, replacing old Spanish leather.
The spacious fireplace is framed by richly carved mahogany.
Its rival as a Richardson fireplace (right) was in Capitol
until 1917 when it was moved with Court of Appeals Chamber.

8. MILLION DOLLAR STAIRCASE

The telegram came as an utter surprise to Isaac Perry. Puzzled, he looked again to be sure he had read the signature correctly. It was: Grover Cleveland, Governor.

The message said that Governor Cleveland would appreciate it if he could come to Albany and see him. Isaac Perry couldn't imagine what for. He never had met Cleveland, and political plums were not his dish.

Mr. Perry was past the age of sixty, and was prospering as a builder and self-trained architect in Binghamton. Some of the most admired buildings in Binghamton and Elmira were his work. His fellow-townsmen respected him, too, for solidity of character. Perry was content where he was.

Still, he did not ignore a summons from the Governor. Perry caught a train for Albany, wondering. He was a brawny, big-statured man with a flowing white beard, and the niceties of personal appearance were not one of his worries. The suit in which he went to see the Governor was dusty and stood in need of pressing. The hat was a battered, wide-brimmed slouch that he wore daily at work.

The anteroom to the Executive Chamber was full of people. The new Governor was creating quite a stir with his "open-door policy." Anyone, within reason, could get in to see him. There was a saying that he might as well set his desk out in front of the Capitol where he could have the extra advantage of fresh air.

Isaac Perry expected to take his turn and have a long wait. But the secretary took a look at his card and ushered him at once into the Chamber, much to the disgruntlement of those ahead. When he departed, the man next in line was admitted and came right to the point. He would like to apply for the newly created post of Commissioner of the Capitol.

"As it happens," the Governor replied, "I have just now made that appointment."

The applicant's jaw dropped. "What! That farmer-looking man?"

"The same." The interview came to an abrupt end.

The reaction of Capitol politicians was much similar. Who was this Perry?—

they wanted to know. The grapevine had it that a certain man from down the Hudson, politically "deserving," was slated for the $7,500 position.

Perry went home to prepare his wife for a move that neither of them especially wanted. The Governor had flung him a challenge he couldn't resist, even though it meant a financial sacrifice. The Capitol had been under construction for fifteen years and was still far from finished. Grover Cleveland wanted him to take sole charge and get it done—hopefully within three years. The Governor's only injunction was to "be as economical as possible . . . but not lose sight of erecting it in a substantial and creditable manner."

So far as the political wiseacres could see, the Governor had picked Isaac Perry out of nowhere. True, he happened to be a Democrat, for voting purposes only. He had pulled no wires, and in fact did not even know the job had been created. In an era when the Capitol project was cynically called a "patronage factory," such an appointment was unheard-of. Perry handed the politicians another jolt by announcing his employment policy: he would hire men on merit alone, and their ability to deliver a fair day's work, regardless of their politics.

The work had been governed by New Capitol Commissions ever since it started. When Governor Cleveland took office in 1883—elected because of his record as the reform mayor of Buffalo—he found that the cost of the Capitol already had exceeded $14,000,000, and he said: ". . . the building should be finished as quickly as practicable, and the delays, errors and expense attending its construction, if possible, forgotten."

The way to do this, he conceived, was to abolish the hydra-headed Commission and substitute a single Commissioner of the Capitol who knew his business. A compliant Legislature passed a bill creating such a position, to be filled by "a suitable person who shall be skilled in the construction of buildings and architectural plans." The Governor signed it the day it was passed, and at the same time—before any political undertow could get going—sent to the Senate his nomination of Isaac G. Perry, which was confirmed.

Quietly in advance, Governor Cleveland had been conducting a confidential search for the right man. From many quarters, he was told of Isaac Perry. Hence the surprise telegram. When the news broke, one reporter was inspired to a bit of doggerel:

> Grover inaugurated the plan;
> He belongs to a future race—
> To let the office seek the man
> Instead of the man the place.

Had Perry foreseen the difficulties of a job so subject to political pressures and legislative vagaries—or that it would take another fifteen years to finish the Capitol —he surely would have thought twice before accepting.

James W. Eaton was dismissed as building superintendent when Perry took over, and he put in the winning bid for tearing down the old Capitol and the State Library that stood beside it.

Governor Cleveland was especially anxious to see the Senate Staircase built without delay. The Assembly Staircase was the only one as yet completed. Perry started the Senate stairs at once. He also removed and rebuilt a great deal of defective masonry. The corridors were dark and ventilation was notoriously bad. Perry went around knocking holes through walls, and hence became known as the man who let light and air into the Capitol.

Perry got on splendidly with the Capitol architects, Eidlitz and Richardson, who continued on an annual retainer basis. At his request, they left their working drawings in his custody. His aim was to carry out their designs faithfully. Still to be

Grand Old Man of the Capitol was Isaac Perry, architect in charge during last years of construction. He favored stone carving in profusion. Below: two of the Governors carved around skylight vault of Great Western Staircase. Both Cornell and Cleveland urged speedier completion of the laggard building. Cleveland appointed Perry.

done for Eidlitz were the Senate Staircase and the central tower; for Richardson, the substitute Court of Appeals courtroom, the Western Staircase, and the Great Gable of the western façade. Then, too, the problem of the Eastern Approach had to be solved, whenever the money was forthcoming with which to do it. As it turned out, this exterior front stairway was Isaac Perry's one distinctly personal contribution to the architecture.

The Senate Staircase carried still further the penchant of Eidlitz for mingling the Moorish-Saracenic note with Victorian Gothic. With the warm cooperation of Perry—who had a keen taste for stone-carving—the architect embroidered the four-story stairs with delicate arabesques. But the intaglios, in this case, were not all purely ornamental, though the casual spectator might think so. Eidlitz did an extraordinarily bold thing. As Richardson characteristically put emotion into his work, Eidlitz infused his with intellect.

Scarcely a quarter-century earlier, Charles Darwin had propounded his theory of evolution. It continued to be a very controversial subject. Eidlitz had the temerity to introduce it into the Senate Staircase. An intricate series of graceful semi-arches climbs the stairway, and they are bordered all the way by arabesques in a series of rectangular frames. No two figures are duplicated. A close inspection will show that the figures portray the ascending scale of evolution, as the stairs go up—from lowly sea life to an elephant and a camel at the top.

Other distinctions went into this classic stairway, which architectural critics praised as one of the most original and vigorous works of the Gothic revival. Long famous—though by no means a unique device—is the nine-foot wheel, or rose-window, in the balustrade between the third and fourth levels. One comes suddenly upon a large heraldic beast perched, with gaping fangs, on a sloping offset. The Gothic arches are adorned with cusps, and all at once the spectator becomes aware that the cusps in some cases are human heads. In such ways did Eidlitz and Perry enjoy themselves with the Senate Staircase.

A special kind of reddish freestone which was particularly adaptable to fine carving was imported from Scotland—Corsehill sandstone. Its advantage was that when first quarried it was rather soft; but it hardened slowly on exposure to the air, and when rubbed down it felt like polished wood. This stone could actually be cut by the carver, rather than hammered. It worked out so well on the Senate Staircase that it became the principal stone for the Great Western Staircase.

The Senate Staircase was completed in 1885 while the Great Western was just being started. Grover Cleveland by then had gone on to the White House. One of the high moments of Isaac Perry's career was when President Cleveland, on an official visit to Albany, called for him and asked to be shown the status of work on the Capitol, especially the finished stairway. At the end of the tour, the President said: "Come down to Washington, Perry, and I'll show you some large and fine buildings, but I won't promise any so handsome or grand as this one."

Meanwhile, Perry had been finishing up the western façade—the most sophisticated face the Capitol has to show to the world. The main feature of this wall is the Great Gable, which, because of its elaborate ornamentation, required a vast amount of skilled labor. Nothing on the exterior of the building so richly repays scrutiny as this gable, measuring over 82 feet at its base and nearly 66 feet high. It is richly carved—even to a pair of winged Babylonian lions—and its tympanum is patterned with raised circles separated by bars. The design for the unique massive finial at its apex was done by Alexander Wadsworth Longfellow (a nephew of the poet), at that time a draftsman for Richardson.

The New York Capitol was one of the first public buildings in the United States to be electrically lighted. The year before Perry's arrival, installation had begun, and "dynamo machines" were put in the basement for the individual power plant. The Commission reported adoption of the Maxim incandescent light—"a steady, clear white light, perfectly natural and easy for the eye, which burns in a hermetically sealed exhausted glass bulb, entirely without combustion, and therefore does not consume the oxygen, or heat or in any manner vitiate the atmosphere." Weston arc-lights flickered in the main corridors. Perry finished the electrification of the Capitol, and reported in 1885 that 940 incandescent lamps were operating, some of them in the legislative chambers.

Perry's troubles began within a year of his appointment when the Legislature made a drastic cut in appropriation and he was faced with laying off 725 men. At that stage, he was naive enough to believe that a personal appeal to the Senate and Assembly would help. Rather plaintively, he said: "I do not wish to be understood as intending or assuming to dictate to the Legislature what appropriations it should make"; but went on: "To discharge the present well organized, excellent and faithful force of granite workers and other mechanics, compelling them to seek employment elsewhere, would not only subject the State to an incalculable loss, and the large number of workmen to great suffering, but would be contrary to true economy."

Perry had gone to great pains to build up a competent, and what he hoped would be a stable, working corps. He could not hold it together if there were periodic interruptions of work—and repeated lay-offs, for lack of funds, were exactly what he now began to encounter. Any prospect for finishing the building in three years went glimmering.

Nevertheless Perry stuck, in defiance of some legislative attempts to get rid of him. In passing an 1886 appropriation bill for the Capitol, the Legislature attached a rider to abolish the position of Commissioner of the Capitol and revert to a board. Governor David B. Hill vetoed the bill for that reason, and leaped angrily to Perry's defense: "He is removed without any charges having been presented against him, in the absence of any investigation or hearing, and in the face of the conceded fact that he is an honest man and a faithful and competent architect and builder."

The bill was not passed over the veto. The Legislature adopted another tactic—that of withholding appropriations. For two successive years, there was no Capitol appropriation at all. Work on the Western Staircase came to a complete standstill. The next strategem was to try to restrict Perry's independence by restoring the Commission system over him. Little by little, the Legislature succeeded in this. But the office of Commissioner of the Capitol remained and he continued to fill it to the end.

Beloved by the men who worked for him, Perry was familiarly known as "the grand old man of the Capitol." He seemed immune to age. His home was on Hawk Street, only a block from his work. The Capitol was his life, and he was to be seen prowling the building at night and on holidays.

The Western Staircase was not far along when its designer, Richardson, died. The architect had allowed for some ornamental carving, but to nowhere near the extent to which Perry carried it. Richardson had no innate objection to carved heads: in fact, several small ones are to be found on the Albany City Hall. But it is a fair guess that Richardson would not have approved turning his majestic stairway into a "stone museum" of portraiture. His plans show that he had intended some life-sized lions on pedestals at the bottom, and female statuary upholding lights near the top. At any rate, Perry made the Great Western Staircase a stone-carvers' paradise.

The Western Staircase is the one popularly nicknamed the Million-Dollar Staircase. It more than deserves the label. The actual cost was in the neighborhood

A detail of Senate Staircase that draws much attention is the wheel, or rose window. This is a Gothic device often seen in European cathedrals. Eidlitz had previously used a rose window in synagogue, Temple Emanu-El, New York Ci[ty]. At right: Senate Staircase as viewed from top level. Grover Cleveland, as Governor, expedited its construction.

As the Senate Staircase mounts upward,
the ascending scale of evolution keeps pace
in arabesque figures bordering semi-arches.
Eidlitz had these carved during a period
when Darwin's theory was highly arguable.
The architect's passion for mingling Oriental
motifs with Gothic is exemplified in stairway.
At left: heraldic beast glares from an offset;
cusps in the arch represent human heads.

of $1,500,000. The stair-well measures 77 by 70 feet, and in height is 119 feet to the skylight. A steam-engine in the attic hoisted the stone for its construction. Aside from the elaborate carvings, the imaginative use of elliptical arches is its distinguishing characteristic.

But it took twice as long to build as it should have. The periodical lay-offs for lack of funds accounted for this. It was begun in 1884. Ten years later, Perry said in a report that the actual working time on it had been five and one-half years. While it was structurally completed in 1897, carving went on a year longer.

Before it was entirely finished, two Governors, Levi P. Morton and Frank S. Black, had walked up the Western Staircase on their way to inauguration.

Then, at long last, money was made available for the Eastern Approach. The "advanced terrace" idea of Eidlitz and Richardson—never more than a tentative proposal—was discarded in favor of a stairway, but a more pretentious one than Fuller had envisioned.

Richardson was dead. Eidlitz had faded out of the picture since the unhappy ceiling affair. Here was Isaac Perry's supreme chance to prove his worth as an architect in his own right. The front staircase—thanks to the workings of time, fate, and the Legislature—was purely Isaac Perry's creation. He designed it in Romanesque style, and yet was not imitative of his predecessors. Not unexpectedly, he turned the stone-carvers loose upon it.

Wise, now, in the ways of politicians, Perry quite deliberately laid the foundations for the entire staircase all at once, instead of doing them piecemeal, and he got granite on top of them as fast as possible. He was not taking any chances of having somebody curtail the dimensions. The stairway was begun in 1891, and was virtually the last thing done on the outside of the building. The steps extend out from the front of the building a distance of 166 feet, seven inches. So far as cost of construction goes, they, too, could accurately be called a Million-Dollar Staircase.

The odd thing about this front staircase is that relatively few people make use of it. Its 77 steps are impractical for the daily business of the Capitol, and many a legislator can truthfully say he never has climbed them.

The final treatment of the east façade presented a problem. Perry proposed to give it a gable in the center, similar to the Great Gable of the west façade. There was to be a 16-foot projection of the front to support it. Doubt as to the capacity of the foundations to hold the weight compelled the abandonment of the gable. Reluctantly, Perry compromised the façade with a set-back balcony over the entrance portico. Instead of the gable, he placed a trio of dormers at the roof's edge.

The "grand old man of the Capitol" was still actively at work at the age of seventy-five, a straight and sturdy figure. It was remarked of him that if he had donned a toga he would have resembled nothing more than a Roman senator. Towards the last, his duties were curtailed when Governor Black placed the superintendent of public works, George Aldridge, in full charge of finishing the Capitol. Perry watched a bit sadly as some of his cherished plans were unceremoniously dropped.

Perry's tenure of office was written into the statutes. The 1883 law creating a Commissioner of the New Capitol stipulated that "said office shall cease" upon completion of the building. The building was declared finished on January 1, 1899.

On that day Theodore Roosevelt became Governor. One of his appointments was that of a State Architect—a post newly created. Governor Roosevelt gave Perry a pat on the back for a job well done, and consigned him to retirement. Perry returned to his old home in Binghamton to live with his memories.

In all its checkered history, no one man had labored so devotedly for so long a term to get the New York Capitol built as Isaac Perry.

Architect's tracing, much-fingered,
for Great Western Staircase (left)
is from files of the State Architect.
It called for female statuary at top and
couchant lions at lower level;
these features did not materialize.
At right: a fascinating glimpse
through arches and branching steps.
Somber anomalous note is struck by
fall-out shelter sign on pillar.
Below: grand sweep of the staircase
is caught by camera from third level,
up-looking. The skylight no longer
serves as such. It was blacked out
during World War II, and afterwards
was replaced with opaque gilt panels.

Front staircase of Capitol (below) was termed the Eastern Approach all the time it was a-building. It was virtually the final touch put upon the edifice in the 1890s. At left: the Capitol as it appeared before the staircase was begun. Side portico had yet to be built as well, on Washington Avenue. Romanesque vaulting (at right) is ceiling of the porte-cochère beneath the eastern staircase. This is where Governors arrive to take up their day's duties. Governor Nelson A. Rockefeller is seen alighting from car.

9. CASE OF THE UNFORTUNATE CEILING

The Assembly Chamber ceiling as it was in all its glory. The center stone was 56 feet above floor of the Chamber. Never before had groined arches been dared with such a span. Ornate patterns were incised and painted in varied hues. Note large visitors' gallery under far arch, that is no more.

Misfortune plagued the wonderful ceiling of Leopold Eidlitz.

After the first cracked stone was replaced, four new cracks appeared. The 1882 Legislature authorized a commission of two architects and a civil engineer to make an independent study of its "safety and durability." These experts decided that the foundations under the four main columns of the Assembly Chamber were loaded to the extreme limit of safety; that unequal settlement had occurred; that "the continued stability of the vaulted ceiling is a matter of doubt"; and that it had been "an error of judgment to erect that most delicate of all architectural devices, a stone groined ceiling, and particularly one of unusual span and weight, on foundations not absolutely secured against uneven settlement." They recommended "with great reluctance" that the architect be instructed to remove all the stone vaulting and substitute a wooden ceiling.

Governor Cornell called a quick conference and showed the report. It was taken for granted that the Assembly would refuse to occupy its Chamber at the next session. In this anticipation, the desks and chairs of members were removed to the Court of Appeals chamber, on the floor below, just then being vacated for the newer courtroom.

The architect rushed to the defense of his work. Eidlitz, Richardson & Company, in a communication to the Governor, took issue with the adverse report, blaming the fractures on the normal settling of a heavy building. They asked, and were granted, permission to make repairs at their own expense. The Assembly took them at their word that the ceiling was then "a perfectly sound and permanent structure." The desks and chairs were moved back.

Obviously, Eidlitz himself continued to worry. More than once during the 1880s he urged the Trustees of Public Buildings to make further repairs affecting the equilibrium of the arches. In May of 1887, he wrote Governor David B. Hill, as chairman of the trustees, asking that a new board of competent experts be appointed to examine the ceiling. "Our professional reputation," he said, "should not be permitted to be assailed, nor should we be held responsible for the integrity of the work while our recommendations to do necessary work for its completion and make necessary repairs for its maintenance are not acted upon."

That same October, a seven-pound chunk of stone was found one morning calmly reposing on the lush red carpet of the Assembly Chamber.

The fall of the stone did not become public knowledge until the Legislature met in January, 1888. Then the repercussions jolted the Capitol, figuratively, to its very foundations. Legislation languished for weeks. The 128 Members of Assembly could think of little else than the tons of rock above their heads, poised, in their vivid imaginations, like the sword of Damocles.

"In my opinion," declaimed Assemblyman Danforth E. Ainsworth of Oswego County, "no Assemblyman can sit in this chamber without the thought of an awful doom, perhaps, before him." Another member said: "This room is now in theory a legislative mausoleum, and will be so soon, in fact, unless we vacate it."

A resolution was introduced to direct the State Superintendent of Insurance to take out a $25,000 insurance policy on the life of each Assemblyman for the duration of the session, the premium to be paid by the State.

The Democratic minority leader, William F. Sheehan of Buffalo, was informed that a stone directly above his seat was dangerously loose. Thereafter he darted into and out of his seat for only a moment at a time. Assemblyman Austin A. Yates, of Schenectady, who sat beneath the massive center stone, candidly admitted: "I am here because I haven't the courage to stay away."

Stereoscopic views were a parlor pastime of the period, and new Capitol was a popular subject, along with Niagara Falls. Assembly Chamber was a stunner when seen in stereoscope. After ceiling began to fall, the Assembly had to vacate while a rough timber structure was hastily erected to hold it for duration of the session. Below: diagram of the bracing.

While a few members were noticeably absent from sessions, most of them either pooh-poohed the danger or espoused the attitude of Mr. Yates. A newspaperman dubbed these brave ones the "Assembly Casabiancas." (Casabianca was the hero of Felicia Hemans' poem that begins: "The boy stood on the burning deck,/ Whence all but him had fled." As the naval battle raged around him, the duty-bound son of the dead Admiral stood there until the fire reached the powder magazine and blew up the ship.)

A New York editorialist satirized the situation. "It is obvious," he wrote, "that the Assemblyman does not want to die in his sins." He suggested that all legislative bodies be "kept in constant fear of death by some artificial means, such as, for instance, a ceiling that was always going to drop, but never did." The stones might even be so arranged as to produce "a mild rumble" whenever a bad bill was introduced.

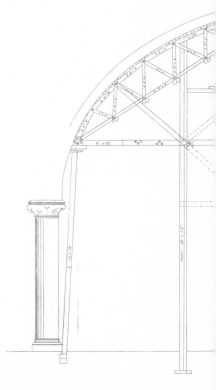

Actually, the danger was real and imminent. Stone-dust sifted down upon desk tops. A member found a rock fragment in his seat. John I. Platt of Poughkeepsie collected the chips that fell until he had a dozen—one "as big as a soup-plate"—in a box under his desk, and then displayed them to his colleagues. A Brooklyn Assemblyman soon was exhibiting an even larger rock, but was strongly suspected of having brought it back from a weekend at home.

After receiving the warning letter from Leopold Eidlitz the previous May, Governor Hill had considered calling a special session of the Legislature, but decided against it because he feared the publicity would excite a "panic" among Assemblymen. The letter was kept secret. Now, with the Assembly back in the Chamber and the spalls tumbling, Eidlitz fired off a really urgent letter to Albany. Since his prior appeals had gone unheeded, said he, "we cannot, in reason, be held responsible for possible accidents." And he went on: "But, inasmuch as, by reason of the long neglect above referred to, such accidents are possible, we deem it our duty to respectfully protest against the further occupancy of the north wing of the Capitol in its present condition; and we request that you will direct that the Assembly Chamber, the State Library and the offices in that part of the building, be closed

until definite action, in accordance with our repeated recommendation, shall have been taken."

With the architect himself hinting darkly of "accidents," the Governor could not longer keep the Legislature uninformed. He summoned committee chairmen of both Houses and laid before them the two Eidlitz letters, remarking that, if he were an Assemblyman, he would not occupy the room a single day. Assemblyman Ainsworth, chairman of the Appropriations Committee, told the Assembly of their existence on January 20.

The Assembly already had a bill in the works for a special commission to study the ceiling once again. Its members would be: State Engineer John Bogart; Thomas C. Clarke, a Poughkeepsie civil engineer; and Richard M. Upjohn, a New York architect. The Senate returned the bill with an amendment to require this commission to submit, with its report, an estimate of the cost of removing the ceiling. This ruffled feathers in the Assembly. An angry debate ensued, in which the Senate was charged with quibbling about a "life-and-death matter," but the bill passed.

The three experts went to work immediately. Entering the loft above the ceiling, they discovered a fresh crack at the apex of the main vault. It was big enough so they could look down and see the floor of the Chamber, 56 feet below. Mr. Upjohn backed away, swearing fervently: "I value my life more than all the Capitols on earth."

Although the commission had been given 40 days in which to prepare its report, it rushed an interim report to the Assembly saying: "We recommend that the Assembly Chamber and the story beneath be immediately evacuated."

The emergency report was read just before a Friday adjournment in early February. A stunned silence ensued. "You could have heard a pin drop," a reporter wrote with unconscious irony.

Upon reconvening Monday night, the legislators had dropped their pose of bravado. Fully half the Assembly seats were vacant. Those members present were looking not so much at the Speaker as at the ceiling. The session lasted exactly 12 minutes. A headline said: "Lawmakers Demoralized."

Next morning many Assemblymen reported with overcoats on and hats in hand, and remained standing. A report was heard that the only other suitable room was the Senate Chamber; and that the Senate—with its much smaller membership—might easily occupy the Assembly Parlor for the nonce. A resolution was sent across to the Senate asking if that body would lend the use of its Chamber to the Assembly.

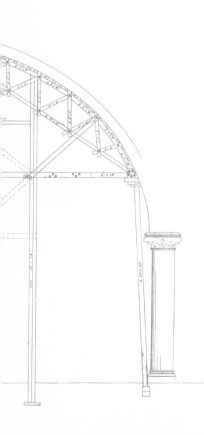

The Senate debated the request very briefly and refused. One Senator made the jocular motion that they place that particular resolution "under the table." His remark was carried back to the Assembly and more feathers were ruffled. It looked as if civil war would erupt momentarily between the two houses of the Legislature. An irate Assemblyman jumped up and proposed that they march over and "take the Senate Chamber by storm."

Finally, amid mutterings about the "selfish Senate," a decision was made to try the Assembly Parlor—a very fine room, but designed only for lounging and committee sessions. The desks were jammed in cheek-by-jowl. A board platform was erected for the Speaker. When the members had shoe-horned themselves into their seats, the clerk stood up and announced with a straight face: "There will be a joint session of the Senate and Assembly in this room in 15 minutes."

It was quickly evident that the wheels of legislation would be greatly hampered by this expedient. All was wild confusion. The worst drawback of all was lack of ventilation. Frequent recesses had to be taken to air out the room.

Meanwhile, Isaac Perry had worked out a scheme for shoring up the ceiling and making the Chamber at least habitable for the remainder of the session. Both

85

houses adjourned for a week and went home while the change was being made.

The Assembly came back to an almost unrecognizable Chamber. One member scanned the room disgustedly and observed: "Looks some like a western town after a séance with a cyclone."

Four pine uprights, braced with criss-crossed beams, upheld a system of latticed wooden trusses which in turn supported the ceiling. The ceiling and trusses were hidden from view by a full plank staging at a height of forty-two feet—just in case a wayward stone should break loose.

As the Assembly at last settled down to work, its members would twitch nervously at an occasional clatter on the staging overhead. It usually turned out that a practical joker had bribed a page boy to go up and drop something on the planks.

Unsightly as these makeshift surroundings were, the Assembly found one decided improvement: the acoustics were very much better!

Leopold Eidlitz, in New York, was deeply distressed, and spoke his thoughts in letters to his surviving partner, Olmsted. He was hopeful that the so-called Bogart Commission would recommend the rebuilding of the ceiling, not its utter removal. "Both Bogart and Clarke tell me that it is their intention to do so," he wrote, "and that so far they see no technical reason why it should not be done." Again: "Our status in Albany and my reputation as an architect measurably depend upon this, and a little friendly influence will do much good at this time. If I am right in thinking that you can personally do much good with Mr. Bogart, I wish you would come on to see him on purpose."

But the battle Eidlitz put up to save his temperamental ceiling was doomed to failure. The Bogart Commission's final report, on April 26, 1888, recommended total elimination of the stone-groined ceiling and its replacement by one of wood or metal. In view of the improved acoustics noted with the temporary plank staging, it was suggested that the new ceiling should be flat.

Serious cracks meanwhile had been found in the Assembly staircase and in the Golden Corridor, as well. The commission recommended extensive repairs for both these Eidlitz show-pieces. The Golden Corridor could not be saved. Within two years, it was demolished and its space partitioned off into committee rooms. (Today the area of the once-celebrated corridor is occupied by the Law Library of the Attorney General's office.)

The Legislature forthwith passed a bill appropriating $278,992—with certain strings attached. It specified that the work of removing the old ceiling and constructing a new one was to be in the complete charge of the superintendent of public buildings, Charles B. Andrews—bypassing the Capitol commissioner, Isaac Perry. Moreover, it established an Assembly Ceiling Committee, which was empowered to employ a special architect for the job, and to award the contract ($40,000 of the appropriation was earmarked for repair of the staircase).

Governor Hill wanted very much to veto the bill. He could see no reason why the work should not be under the control of the regular Capitol architect, Mr. Perry; and he was suspicious that the Ceiling Committee would be an entering wedge towards getting Perry back under the thumb of a Commission. "Such a committee," said he in his accompanying message, "not infrequently constitutes the worst kind of a commission, and oftentimes leads to deals, jobs, abuses and corruption. . . . An emergency is presented. If I refuse to approve this bill the Assembly ceiling must remain in its present disgraceful, if not dangerous, condition, for another year and during another session. . . . The bill is only permitted to become a law because of the extraordinary existing situation."

Governor Hill must be credited with remarkable foresight. The legislative stage was now set for the unhappy sequel.

*The new ceiling was flat and lower.
Architectural dissonance is seen
in the way it cuts top of arch;
also in clear fact that granite
pillars were designed to uphold
a far nobler structure than this.
Coffer panels were papier mâché
moulded to mimic carved oak. Less
permissible was the use
of same material in spandrels.*

Charles Andrews had few discernible qualifications for being superintendent of public buildings. An investigator later referred to him as "virtually the janitor of this building." The Ceiling Committee allowed him $3,500, on top of his regular salary, for supervising the ceiling job. And it left it to Mr. Andrews to get bids on the contract.

Andrews brought in six bids for the Committee's action. The lowest was $270,150, submitted by an Albany building contractor, John Snaith, later revealed as a close personal friend of Andrews. Only in retrospect did it occur to anyone how close the bid was to the actual appropriation, with enough margin to cover Andrews' extra pay and the fee of a special architect.

It was Andrews who recommended such an architect to the Ceiling Committee—one Arthur H. Rowe, who, he said, was a professor of architecture at Cornell University. Rowe had indeed been on the Cornell faculty for a short time, but was dismissed when the university discovered he had obtained the post with false credentials. At any rate, the Committee engaged Mr. Rowe, and he it was who drew the plans for the new ceiling—and later altered them, at Andrews' behest.

An intriguing bit of coincidence enters here. John Snaith had been one of the fourteen "building trade mechanics" imported from England in 1869 by Ezra Cornell to build a home for him on the fringe of the Cornell University campus. At that time he spelled his name Sneath. Another of those British artisans was Louis J. Hinton, who will be encountered later in these pages as foreman of stone-carvers on the Western Staircase. Snaith settled in Ithaca as a contractor, and had relocated in Albany just prior to the ceiling affair. He and Hinton were doing work on the Capitol, then, at the same time.

After awarding the contract to John Snaith, the Assembly Ceiling Committee adjourned and went home. Not one of its five members came near Albany all that summer of 1888 to see how the work was progressing.

Snaith sub-contracted the Assembly Staircase repair job to Timothy J. Sullivan, another Albany contractor, who likewise turned out to be a bosom friend of Andrews. (Before it was all over, this trio of Snaith, Sullivan, and Andrews would be depicted as "a closed corporation.")

The magnificent ceiling had lasted precisely ten years. Now the stone was stripped from its gracefully arched vaults and carted off to find its way into various Albany buildings—all of which were Snaith contracts. In its place, but fourteen feet lower, a flat wooden ceiling was carpentered in—quite similar in appearance to the Senate ceiling. It sealed off forever the renowned Hunt murals. While this new ceiling was ornamental enough, with its carved oak beams and deep-sunk coffers, it was architecturally incongruous. It cut the tops of arches and was too low over the tiers of stained-glass windows. The ponderous granite pillars were never intended to uphold so mild a structure.

When the 1889 Assembly convened in the remodelled Chamber, the members at least did not have to fret about anything falling on their heads, and they were overjoyed to find how much more clearly they could hear one another speak. But another kind of trouble was brewing. Its nature was hinted in a newspaper dispatch: "The Assemblymen have resolved to learn whether their new doll, the reconstructed Assembly Chamber, is made of sawdust or not."

A rumor had spread into the hinterlands to the effect that plaster of paris—not carved oak—had gone into the ceiling. A Saratoga Springs legislator had taken a reconnoitering trip to Albany while the work was in progress and spirited away a strip of ornamental beading. Triumphantly he now pulled it forth and passed it around to his associates, declaring: "As any member can see, it is made of plaster of paris. . . . There isn't a particle of carved oak in that ceiling!"

Legislators and taxpayers alike were by this time so hypersensitive to the Assembly ceiling that they were ready to believe anything said of it. Axiomatically, another investigation was in order. The Committee on Appropriations was to conduct it. More experts were hired. Loose statements got into print to the effect that the alleged plaster of paris was starting to crumble already, and that soon the entire ceiling would be "coming down like snowflakes."

The truth was that plaster of paris was not the material; that nothing was beginning to flake; and that the Saratoga legislator was wrong in saying there was no carved oak in the ceiling. The frames of the panels were of carved oak, but the sunken coffers were of moulded papier mâché, painted to resemble oak. When the inquiry disclosed this, the public got the impression that papier mâché was a flimsy product that would rapidly fall apart. In reality, it was a quite durable and reputable material that was widely used at the time in ornamental architecture. Nor was it cheap, compared to wood. The ceiling of the Metropolitan Opera House was cited as one example of the use of papier mâché.

Superintendent Andrews readily admitted the papier mâché coffers, stating that the specifications of the contract allowed a choice between it and quartered oak; that he and the contractor had chosen papier mâché because it would better withstand the heat of the room rising to the ceiling; that oak coffers would soon have cracked at the habitual 70° temperature. Snaith, on the stand, said: "It is decidedly the best and most substantial ceiling in the Capitol."

As a matter of fact, those papier mâché panels survived very well. They remained in the ceiling until the mid-1930s, without noticeable disintegration, and were then replaced with plain uncarved wood.

The issue was not so much the fact of the papier mâché as it was whether or not the specifications had permitted the alternative. This question never was settled satisfactorily. The written specifications produced at the inquiry said: "The panels are to be quartered oak, as shown, properly glued up and finished, or of papier-mâché, as may be directed by the superintendent." Only one of the five members of the Ceiling Committee testified that he could remember seeing the words "papier mâché" in the specifications at the award of the contract. When all was said, a dual question was left dangling: either the other four members of the committee had not bothered to read the specifications; or someone had tampered with the specifications after the contract was awarded.

The Appropriations Committee reported on February 25. It found the Assembly Ceiling Committee to have been guilty of "gross carelessness," but laid the principal blame at the door of the Legislature itself for having entrusted the direction of the job to "a confessedly incompetent man, and inexperienced committee . . . to the exclusion of the competent state officer [i.e., Isaac Perry]." It conceded that the contract did permit the alternative between oak and papier mâché. The report charged that the architect, Rowe, had made changes in the plans during the course of the work, under Andrews' instructions, and that the changes were always in the direction of greater profits for the contractors; for instance, the number of panels was reduced from the specified 768 to 396. It criticized Andrews for "negligence in not properly supervising the work and insisting upon strict compliance with the contract." It recommended that the Ceiling Committee refuse to accept the ceiling as it stood; that the duties of Andrews be transferred to Perry, who should then compel the contractor to make good on his short-cuts.

The board of experts (whose architect members were Stanford White and Archimedes Russell) had reported in the meantime, finding that the papier mâché was "eminently suited for the vaulted panels"; but that the contractor had been remiss in other respects, such as using that material for the spandrels and beading.

The words "Papier mache or oak" penned on tracing for spandrels of new ceiling suggest a choice. This drawing was an exhibit during the investigations. Hamilton Fish, Jr., below left, headed one of the inquiries, Danforth E. Ainsworth the other. Despite the uproar, accused contractors went scot-free.

The dynamite in their report was the estimate they made of the actual value of the work accomplished—$165,000, allowing for a fair profit. This meant that Snaith and company had made a profit of $106,000.

Some Assemblymen felt that the report of the Appropriations Committee was too weak, especially in its slap-on-the-wrist for Andrews. The Legislature already had sent a resolution to the Trustees of Public Buildings urging the suspension of Andrews on grounds of dereliction of duty—but the Trustees held off acting upon it. Determined not to let the matter drop, the Assembly named a special committee to carry on a second, more thorough, inquiry, one object of which was to ascertain into what "channels" Snaith's alleged $106,000 profit had flowed. The chairman of this committee was Assemblyman Hamilton Fish, Jr., of Putnam County.

When the Fish Committee opened its hearings on March 4, it found itself embarrassingly short of key witnesses. Snaith and Rowe were absent from the city. Snaith's bookkeeper was reported as being in Bermuda "for his health." A local jeweler wanted for questioning also had taken a sudden trip to Bermuda (it was said that he had sold an expensive piece of jewelry to Snaith as a gift for Mrs. Andrews). Mrs. Andrews, when sought, was reported to be visiting relatives in Boston; later evidence indicated she was actually hidden in the Albany home of a brother.

John Snaith was located in Philadelphia, whither he had fled with a gripsack full of ledgers and account books. Arthur Rowe turned up in Memphis, Tennessee, after visiting Snaith in Philadelphia. Neither could be extradited, the inquiry not being a court of law, and they would not return voluntarily.

The Fish Committee took what testimony it could, and reported in May, with a conclusion that "Andrews, Sullivan and Snaith combined to defraud the people of the State," and that the profit on the contract had been nearer to $120,000. It recommended the removal of Andrews from his state office; called the attention of the district attorney to the evidence it had taken, suggesting that he lay it before a Grand Jury; and prodded the Attorney General to start action against the three men to recover money "of which they have despoiled the state."

The Assembly had craved a stronger report, and now had it. Inexplicably, the legislators voted to reject it, and to accept instead the prior report of the Appropriations Committee. This vacillating behavior prompted a newspaper headline: "Fish Inquiry In Vain."

A fortnight later John Snaith appeared back in town, driving his phaeton coolly through the streets of Albany. A reporter noted that he was "not in the least puffed up by his national notoriety, just the same simple John Snaith, ready to take a state contract, that he ever was."

Not only was Snaith back—he filed a claim against the state for $40,000. This was the amount of the final payment on his contract which the state had withheld when the ceiling scandal erupted.

Andrews was superseded as superintendent of public buildings on June 1, 1889. Two successive Albany County grand juries failed to find indictments against the trio.

That autumn, Attorney General Charles F. Tabor started an action in Oneida County against Snaith, Sullivan, and Andrews to recover $250,563 as damages "occasioned by fraud in repairing the State Capitol." The defendants won a change of venue back to Albany County. Before the case got on the calendar, the Appellate Court granted a motion vacating the order for their arrest.

Snaith's claim for $40,000 against the state was finally disallowed by the Board of Claims. His profit, at least, was reduced by so much.

10. THE TOWER THAT NEVER WAS

Among long-neglected scrolls in State Architect's office was uncovered this tracing for front elevation of Capitol. Evidently current in the 1890s, it provided for grandiose tower that was intended to the last. Also to be remarked is plan for a superb gable on front, similar to the Great Gable of the façade on west side.

It was taken for granted that there must be something impressive sticking up on top. A Capitol without a dome would be as preposterous as a church without a steeple.

Albany at that time was a city of domes. The City Hall had a fine dome, and so did the adjacent State Hall. The existing Capitol and the Albany Academy had their graceful cupolas. A downtown hotel was splendidly domed.

At least some of the competitive plans for a new Capitol were original enough to be domeless. The Commissioners of the Land Office, who held a veto power, made it plain that they would approve no design without a dome. Therefore Thomas Fuller and Arthur Gilman gave them a jim-dandy, on paper. It would spear the sky at 320 feet, and then there would be a castiron eagle or a statue of somebody on the apex. It would be "the landmark of the capitol city." Venturesome sightseers would be able to climb spiral stairs to an observation platform where they would get a stunning view. It was so high in theory that it always was referred to as a tower rather than a dome.

The grand tower was to be placed toward the front (or east side) of the building. It would make an end-wall for the central court. Its dimensions where it passed up through the building would be 66 by 66 feet. The solid granite walls at that stage were nine feet thick. From the entrance floor, visitors could stand in a rotunda, designated in the floor-plans as Tower Hall, and look up a clear seventy-five feet to a concave frescoed ceiling.

As fast as the outer walls grew, so did the ponderous walls to support the tower. Its footings were sunk seven feet deeper than the rest. The granite blocks going into its foundation averaged four tons in weight. The blocks were "stepped out" at the base, giving its walls a pedestal twenty feet wide. There was to be no skimping here!

Then came the Advisory Board. While Eidlitz, Richardson and Olmsted had a good deal to say about the tower, they did not propose to eliminate it. But they doubted if its shape "will long be regarded as entirely felicitous." They drew a new plan making it stubbier and rounder, and giving it a German Romanesque flavor. They deplored the fact that the tower was not located above some room or central space "of specially noble character," or at least a more ample rotunda. It was, in effect, "an edifice by itself."

Prof. Charles Eliot Norton of Harvard, in his exchange of letters with Olmsted during the "Battle of the Styles," expressed himself on the subject:

"I regret the necessity of the dome. It is unmeaning, has no aesthetic or constructive relation with the main building, but is a mere piece of very costly show. It will be a permanent monument not of culture but of barbarism. . . . I suppose the work had gone so far that you were forced to retain this too conspicuous feature— and, being so, you certainly have given it a very effective form, and one not incongruous with the rest of the building."

Construction of the tower was assigned to Eidlitz when, for practical purposes, he and Richardson divided the building between them.

Many stone-cutters worked on it exclusively. By the mid-'90s, its thick granite walls stood twenty feet above the roofline. A shed protected the opening from the elements. Nearly $1,000,000 had been spent upon it. Until then, nobody had done any audible worrying about its weight.

Isaac Perry, the resident Capitol architect, at that time submitted to the Commission a plan for finishing the tower—"based upon the theory that no more weight can be added to the foundation on which the tower as constructed to its present altitude rests." Perry had made a fresh study and decided that the weight, as far as it had gone, was "equivalent to the full sustaining capacity of the earth on which the area of the lowest base course foundations rest."

His proposed solution was to take off the top twenty-six feet of granite and substitute for the rest of the tower a structural steel skeleton, covered with sheet copper and cast bronze ornaments. The weight of the metallic structure, he estimated, would about equal the weight of the granite removed.

Governor Levi P. Morton had just taken office, and, as Governors were wont to do, had appointed a new Capitol Commission. One of its members was a Syracuse architect with the classical name of Archimedes Russell. The Commission was supposed to complete the Capitol without further ado. Mr. Russell took a look at Perry's tower plan and snorted:

"This method of procedure may be of doubtful expediency, venturesome and experimental in an artistic and aesthetic sense, liable perhaps to severe criticism as a cheap and unsubstantial treatment of the crowning feature."

Hurry and economy were now the watchwords. The Commission thought it over and determined that the best thing to do with the tower was get rid of it altogether. Perry's speculations about the weight provided an excellent excuse.

The Commission, in 1896, advertised for bids for removing the temporary roof of the tower, lopping off the protruding part of its walls, putting a permanent roof over the space, and extending the floors of the Capitol right through the tower. The added floor area afforded "valuable and much desired apartments in each story." The fourth story was made into Senate committee rooms.

The third level was "handsomely fitted up" for the newspapers and the telegraph and telephone companies. It also was given a "commodious café." In more recent years, the restaurant was converted into the Legislative Correspondents' Room.

While the legend has come down that the tower was abandoned because the ground beneath would not support its weight, one cannot resist the thought that

Ponderous foundations for the tower were commenced
at same time as building proper. They may be seen as
the inside square in construction photo above.
Below: a section through the proposed tower plan;
note spiral staircase to outlook platform, at top.
At left: the Legislative Correspondents' Room
is within the space of tower, as its walls reveal.
Floors of all levels were projected through.
Right: the "stump" of the tower. The eastern wall
of Central Court displays where it was lopped off.

perhaps a more powerful reason was economy. In reporting its elimination, the Capitol Commission itself left a subtle hint for posterity to ponder: "While all this has been accomplished, it has not been done at the sacrifice or denial of the privilege of yet obtaining the grand metal tower should future generations command the courage to attempt it."

After all, the tremendous weight of the granite walls that were constructed for it, then left uncrowned, has been standing there all these years without catastrophe.

A quarter of a century passed. Under Governor Alfred E. Smith a project was born to restore at least the lower part of the tower space to something like its original concept. The adventitious second floor would be removed to create a rotunda forty feet high. This would then become the Flag Room—repository of the Civil War keepsakes of the State Military Museum. The rotunda would have an arched ceiling with paintings of the historic wars in which New York State has participated. The estimated cost of this improvement was $350,000.

A New York artist, William DeLeftwich Dodge, was commissioned to paint the murals at a fee of $42,000. He spent five years putting the twenty-four panels on canvas in his home studio, aided by his daughter, Sara, while erection of the domed ceiling was delayed. Finally in 1928 the ceiling was ready and the murals were attached. The center-piece was an embossed female figure representing New York State mourning her war dead. Governor Franklin D. Roosevelt dedicated the paintings.

But the floor beneath them had not been removed. It never was. The Great Depression struck and another fine scheme went begging. The space was converted into a mail-and-messenger room for the Executive Department. There the Dodge murals remained unknown to the public—an ornate and expensive ceiling for a clerical staff to work beneath. The paintings never were viewed in the perspective for which they were designed.

Early in 1964, as this book was going to press, preliminary steps were being taken to bring the neglected pictorial ceiling into public view at last. The mailroom was preparing to move elsewhere, giving up its quarters to be redecorated and made a part of the Military Museum after all, even though the floor remains.

Down in the catacombs, the tremendous, stepped-out foundation walls of the Tower that Never Was are imperishable. The dungeon-like square space enclosed by them is used as a padlocked storage room.

The abandoned tower almost got this rotunda during the '20s. Governor Alfred E. Smith nurtured project to remove floor and create tall room for state flag collection. It went as far as painting of war scenes on ceiling by muralist Dodge (below right), who collected $42,000 fee. The depression intervened, and plan went unrealized. Below: visitors inspect relics in Military Museum.

11. THE STONE CARVERS

Stone carving art reached zenith in Capitol. Architects had not believed until then that granite could be carved with such extreme delicacy. Photo from south colonnade of the Eastern Approach shows some of the disproofs: The head at left is Liberty. Higher, above the baluster, is lush figure called Plenty.

A building with so voracious an appetite for granite demanded an army of stone-cutters. Year after year, these men comprised roughly half of the Capitol's working force. Their numbers rose to a peak of 600, and even during the depression 1870s they earned $5 for a 10-hour day, twice the wage of common labor. They were drawn largely from quarry communities, many following the granite from New England. A considerable number shifted to Albany after working on the national Capitol in Washington. The Scottish strain ran strong among them.

These were a breed of men unto themselves, proud in their work and inclined to be clannish. They even had their special occupational hazard—the dread silicosis that came with breathing too much granite dust. The Capitol being the long-enduring job it was, the stone-cutters tended to settle and make homes in Albany, and many brought up families in the city and married them off before the building was completed. The surrounding stone-sheds were a familiar part of the Capitol scene. This was before the day of pneumatic tools, and the mallet and chisel were the standard instruments of the trade.

The stone-cutting army produced an élite corps—the stone carvers. Among these were a few who could be ranked as true architectural sculptors, and two or three who so sharpened their talent by working on the Capitol that they afterwards opened private studios. Thanks to the carvers—and to the fact that Isaac

Perry doted on carving—this building, in certain parts, is an amazing repository of what has since become practically a lost art.

The majority of the carvings, and especially the portraiture, were created during the 1890s, in the terminal phases of construction. Their great outpourings were on the Western (or Million-Dollar) Staircase and the Eastern Approach. The earlier planning did not contemplate any such lavish display. Thomas Fuller, in his 1875 report to the Legislature, emphasized that "all carved work has been omitted." Eidlitz introduced some decorative incised work in the Assembly Chamber, but his Assembly Staircase was relatively chaste. When it came to the Senate Staircase, a good deal more carving was allowable. But it remained for Isaac Perry to carry the carving idea to the ultimate in the two later stairways. In general, the sculptured likenesses of the Western Staircase are historical, those of the front stairway symbolical.

Not everyone at the time wholeheartedly approved of Perry's carving fetish. Archimedes Russell, the architect member of the Capitol Commission in the mid-'90s, ventured the thought in an official report that perhaps the "decorative features" of the Eastern Approach were being "applied indiscriminately and so profusely as to surfeit and disgust the sensibilities."

At any rate, it cannot be gainsaid that the stone carvers of America enjoyed their last unalloyed field-day on the Capitol at Albany. The taste for that type of ornamentation in public buildings waned soon after.

If Perry had prayed for the ideal man to abet him, he could not have been better answered than with the appearance of Louis J. Hinton. Returning to this country in 1885 after several years in his native England, Hinton applied for work on the Capitol just as the Great Western Staircase was beginning to shape up. Perry engaged him as foreman of carvers on that staircase (his pay at the start was $8 a day). Later Hinton took on the added duty of designing all the purely decorative carving. "I was kept busy making free-hand scale drawings," he reminisced in after years, "and laying out the work on the smooth finished surface of the moldings, while still directing the carvers at their work."

Variety was the invincible rule on that staircase. Not even the smallest of decorative themes could be repeated in two different locations. For the sake of authenticity, Hinton hiked about the countryside collecting foliage and flowers for his designs—roses, clematis, trumpet-vine, tulips, passion-flowers, lilies, and grape vines.

Louis Hinton was born in London, the son of a master carver who had worked on the Nelson statue in Trafalgar Square. The boy grew up to be an expert in ecclesiastical carving. In 1869, he was one of a group of fourteen hand-picked "building trade mechanics" brought from England by Ezra Cornell to erect a home for him at Ithaca, N. Y. When that job was done, Hinton worked on terraces and fountains of New York's Central Park, helped Chicago to rebuild after the fire, then, partly because of the depressed economic condition of the United States, went back to England.

The place he found at the Capitol resulted in Albany's becoming his permanent home. Perry trusted him implicitly. Hinton's attitude towards Perry was put in writing many years afterwards: "It is one of my very pleasant memories to have known and loved him. Mr. Perry paid close attention to the carving. I know that not a stone was carved nor an idea carried out in model form or otherwise without the commissioner being in on it from start to finish. He loved the work and passed more time with the men, carving and modeling, than is usual with architects."

Perry's rapt interest in the carvings, and his rigid standards for them, are reflected in the specifications for a contract (in 1895) to complete the upper portions

*Louis J. Hinton was foreman
of carvers on Western stairs.
The pencil portrait of him
was made by his son, Charles,
who also worked on carvings.
Below, from his sketch-book, is
one of Hinton's foliage
designs for the staircase.
He also created spandrel
corbels for medallion
portraits of Governors;
an example seen at right.*

of the Western Staircase:

"The carving of the corbels, cornices and label moldings is to have deep sinkages and be made free and bold, in accordance with the full-size plaster models.

"There must be no feeling of monotony in the design and much variety must be obtained in the decorative work.

"Great care is to be taken in carving the heads, as well as the foliage. The whole work is to be cut deep, clean and sharp, so that the light and shadow will be satisfactory to the capitol commissioner."

The Corsehill freestone, imported from Scotland, gave the carvers an advantage because of its soft workability when fresh from the quarry (it hardened after exposure to the air). Hinton had this to say about the stone: "The material being sandstone, it could be carved much freer than granite, that has to be pounded—not cut—into the required shape."

Perry never missed an opportunity to praise his carvers in his reports. For example: "The artistic workmen who have so lovingly wrought out the designs furnished them have surpassed their previous efforts in the way of good work and deserve high praise, if we do but remember how rare is the faculty they have displayed in these days of hurried competitive work."

For the most part, the carvings were done from models carefully moulded in advance and copied by the carvers with exactitude. But this was not always the case. Hinton was authority for the statement that much of the work was "carved without models, saving the state treasury a very considerable sum." In the instances where the heads were of historical personages or actual living people, the models were made from photographs or paintings.

The Western Staircase is a gallery of great Americans, ranging from Washington, Jefferson, Hamilton, and Franklin, to literary and political figures who were contemporary with the work. The fact that the Civil War was still vivid in the nation's memory while the Capitol was being erected is abundantly exemplified in the carvings. Not only are the standard heroes of that conflict depicted in lifelike sculpture—Abraham Lincoln and Generals Grant, Sherman, and Sheridan. The staircase also enshrines the fanatical John Brown; Harriet Beecher Stowe, who helped to foment the war with "Uncle Tom's Cabin"; and Frederick Douglass, the mulatto who escaped from slavery to become a powerful abolitionist orator. In what the Capitol guides like to refer to as the "Poets' Corner" are to be found Walt Whitman, Longfellow, Whittier, and Bryant. Invention and science are personified in Robert Fulton and Joseph Henry. A prominent position is given to the head of J. V. L. Pruyn, an influential member of the original Capitol Commission.

A considerable number of the heads are anonymous, including a liberal sprinkling of children and a few elderly couples. In a descriptive passage, Isaac Perry said: "There are also many, though smaller heads carved throughout the staircase that have been introduced for artistic effect, to vary the foliage wherever it was deemed suitable. They differ from the larger heads . . . in being merely decorative and not portraiture."

Perry may have made that statement before some of the lesser carvings were put in. Legend has persisted down the years that the unidentified heads represent relatives or friends of the carvers. The legend is supported by the fact that, during the preparation of this book, a half-dozen of the "unknowns" were positively identified.

Two of them were members of Perry's own family: his daughter, Alice, and granddaughter, Lucretia. The mother and daughter were carved separately but in the same side corridor of the staircase, on the third level. They were identified (in 1963) by the granddaughter herself, Mrs. William G. Phelps, Jr., of Binghamton.

(Text continued on page 111)

A New York sculptor modelled historic faces that populate the Great Western Staircase. He was Otto R. Baumgartel, center figure in above group. Plaster models were shipped, put on exhibit before carving. Some literary personalities were included, such as Cooper: satellite heads are characters out of Leatherstocking Tales.

Killian Drabold, a virtuoso
stone carver, pictured at work
on whiskers of Longfellow.
Softness of the sandstone
when fresh from the quarry
aided carvers in attaining
fine detail; stone later
hardened in exposure to air.
Another head in the gallery
known as the Poets' Corner
is that of Walt Whitman (right).
Drabold moved family to Albany
while employed on Capitol,
carved his two young daughters
on the Western Staircase.
Luxuriance of the carvings
is suggested in strip view.

HARRIET BEECHER STOWE.

SUSAN B. ANTHONY

*Almost as an afterthought, someone
realized that no important women
were immortalized on the staircase.
Hastily, a half-dozen were added.
The name of Harriet Beecher Stowe,
author of "Uncle Tom's Cabin,"
still loomed large in public esteem,
and so she merited a niche.
Woman suffrage was in the air,
and the choice of Susan B. Anthony,
feminist leader, was inevitable.
As a nod to Revolutionary history,
Molly Pitcher was enshrined.
Perforce, Molly's is an idealized
face, but they made her winsome.*

One of finest heads sculptured
on *Western Staircase* is this
of *Roger Sherman, a signer*
of *Declaration of Independence.*
Other signers so honored are
Franklin, Jefferson, Schuyler,
George Read and Robert Morris.
All the rest have their names cut
on shields. Viking vessel at
top of bas-relief panels
strikes theme of exploration.
Others depict various aspects of
American life: a log-cabin
schoolhouse in forest clearing;
and a farmer behind his plow.

The fact that the Capitol was being constructed
in the lingering shadow of the Civil War
is reflected again and again in its carvings.
Abraham Lincoln and U. S. Grant share a pillar.
Frederick Douglass (right), an escaped slave,
was famed as orator for the abolitionist cause.
Elsewhere on Western Staircase one may locate
John Brown, Generals Sherman, Sheridan, Scott.

108

FRED. DOUGLAS

*Isaac Perry had a granddaughter, Lucretia.
A childhood pose of her is seen above.
As boss of the Capitol, he had a carver
put her piquant face among the ornaments.
The girl grew up and became the lady
pictured here, Mrs. William Phelps, Jr.,
of Binghamton, N. Y. While this book
was in preparation, she came to Albany
and pinpointed her likeness, at right.*

110

(Text continued from page 100) Along towards the completion of the staircase, complaints were heard that too many of the heads were less historical than political, and not worthy of being so honored. In response to this criticism, under Governor Black's administration several were removed.

About that time, too, someone made the embarrassing discovery that no historically important women had been included among the subjects. George W. Aldridge, the superintendent of public works whom Governor Black had assigned to finish the Capitol, hastily ordered the addition of six women: Molly Pitcher, the heroine who served as a soldier in the Revolution; Mrs. Stowe, the author; Susan B. Anthony, the feminist leader; Clara Barton and Elmina P. Spencer, both Civil War nurses; and Frances E. Willard, the temperance crusader.

Another last-minute addition was the carving of spandrel corbels around the wall surfaces just beneath the skylight dome, with medallion profiles of all Governors of New York State up to and including Frank Black. The corbels were designed by Louis Hinton. As for the Governors, Perry explained: "Great care was taken to insure likeness in each case. Photos were obtained from authentic paintings of those who have passed beyond, those of our past Governors still with us were communicated with and kindly sent pictures that models were made from, for the carvers to copy. Blocks are left with space for six future Governors if posterity deems fit, as time rolls the meshes of his web, to have them carved therein."

Models for the historic portraits of the Western Staircase were made in a New York studio, under contract, by a professional sculptor newly arrived as an immigrant from Germany. He was Otto Richard Baumgartel. As he completed them, Baumgartel would ship the models to Albany, where they were placed on exhibit in the Capitol corridors pending their translation into stone.

Baumgartel was born in 1863, in Saxony, Germany, where he learned the art of wood-carving in his youth. Later he studied sculpture in Berlin. He landed in New York about 1890, and found employment in the studio of Philip Martiny. How he came to do the models for the State Capitol is not precisely clear; his daughter says he was working for someone else at the time. Subsequently, Baumgartel had his own New York studio, and did the sculpture for both Grand Central and Penn Stations in that city. By sheer coincidence, he spent the last decade of his life (1930-40) in Albany, because his daughter by that time lived there. Frequent walks took him to the Capitol where he whiled away many hours examining the sculptures he had helped to create.

Louis Hinton had died a few years before Baumgartel came to Albany, so it is questionable if the two men ever met. While he was foreman of carvers at the Capitol, Hinton had placed his artistically gifted son, Charles, to work among them. "You did lovely carving," he afterwards assured him. Father and son also worked together on carvings in the Albany Cathedral of All Saints. Charles Hinton had a career as an artist and sculptor, with a studio in Bronxville.

One of the chief carvers on the Western Staircase was Killian Drabold, then in his early thirties, who moved his family from New York to Albany for the duration of the work. German-born, in Bavaria, Drabold was brought to America at the age of three. When he had two young daughters of his own, he immortalized them by carving their puckish heads on the Great Western Staircase, one on either side of the dignified physiognomy of Amasa J. Parker. (Parker was a sometime justice of the Supreme Court, Congressman, and a power in the Democratic machine called the Albany Regency).

The nearby carving of Perry's little granddaughter, Lucretia, is markedly similar in style to those of Drabold's daughters. This makes it a logical assumption that Drabold also did that one, in an understanding with Perry.

Near the Capitol, on Washington Avenue, lived Mr. and Mrs. David Saxe, and they had an unusually beautiful child, Sanford. The angelic features of this little boy, less than two years old, attracted the notice of some of the stone-carvers —or so the story goes—and they asked permission of the parents to carve him on the staircase. It was done. Sanford Saxe grew up to be a linen importer and manufacturer of handkerchiefs in New York City.

Killian Drabold returned to New York to live, and his descendants say he helped to carve the lions in front of the New York Public Library.

Among the carvers under Hinton's supervision was a young man named John Francis Brines who showed such promise that Hinton brought him to the attention of Isaac Perry. After watching him work, Perry asked: "Could you make new designs, and superintend the cutting of this work?" Eagerly, he replied: "Yes, Mr. Perry, I could and I'd like the chance."

Perry placed Brines in command of the carvers on the Eastern Approach and of designing and modelling its subjects.

John Brines came from Westerly, Rhode Island, where he was born in 1860. His family being poor, and there being then no child-labor laws, he was sent to work as a mere boy in the granite quarries on the outskirts of town. He displayed so great an aptitude for carving and for modelling designs that his employers promoted him to monument carving. He married a Providence girl in 1889, and they lived for periods at the Gettysburg Battlefield while he worked on a monument, and at Hartford, Connecticut, where he did more carving.

Brines was hired at the Capitol in 1892, just after work had commenced on the Eastern Approach. Perry was on the lookout for a man who could supervise the carving on that staircase. When he took over that job, Brines remembered his old friends back in Westerly, and found places for out-of-work carvers at the Capitol.

Brines spent eight years in Albany. He set up a studio in a shed on the grounds, where the designing and modelling were done for all the carvings on the great terraced approach. In general, he picked the subjects himself, under Perry's watchful eye.

Until that time, architects had not believed that really delicate carving could be done in granite. Brines confounded them with carvings of astonishingly fine detail. The white granite from Hallowell, Maine, lent itself admirably to nuances of the chisel. The largest, most dazzling examples of intricate carving anywhere about the Capitol are the two almost-bacchanalian designs—"Plenty" and "Progress"—over the entrances to the porte-cochère by which New York's Governors arrive at the Capitol.

Semicircular balustraded platforms jut out from the landing nearest the top of the staircase and are supported by 20-ton blocks of granite, rounded and elaborately carved about their circumference. The head of Jupiter is centered on one of these blocks, that of Mercury on the other. These were described by Perry as being "the largest pieces of granite carving in this country."

Symbolism connected with American life and ideals was favored by Brines, and he peopled the staircase with personifications of liberty, literature, science and art; a farmer, a mechanic, a manufacturer. There is an Indian sachem; and also a remarkably eloquent head of a Negro, representing emancipation of the slaves: a chain is about his chest, with the middle link broken.

Perhaps Brines' choicest figures on the front staircase are his native American animals and birds—a wildcat, a raccoon, an owl, a raven, a wolf, a fox, a bison, a turkey, some eagles.

Brines, like Hinton, preferred authentic models for his wild-life designs. Accompanied by an assistant from his modelling shop, William G. Van Zant, he went

John Francis Brines was chief of carvers on front stairway. In photo below, he appears fourth from the left, standing beside bearded Isaac Perry with carvings as backdrop. At right is most elaborate carving on entire building: feminine figure upholding a trellis rich with grapes is symbolic of "Plenty."

out one day into the Pine Bush west of the city looking for a wild turkey. They searched fruitlessly all afternoon. Then, driving back into town, they found their "model"—a domesticated turkey—roosting in a tree in the yard of a brewery.

"In the case of the animals and birds which were carved on the building," Van Zant recollected in later years, "we sought to leave a permanent record of some of the animals and birds common to the earlier period of the country, and this state." (A notable exception to that aim is the head of a lion!)

Van Zant reminisced further: "In the case of each carving, whether it was on the outside of the building, or on the staircase, it was done from a model, and those models were prepared in Mr. Brines' office. Frequently we did not see the completed work at all. The models were turned over to the carvers and they inscribed the figures as it was given to them."

Among carvers who worked on the Eastern Approach were Eugene Baldy, Richard Brines, and George Cruickshank.

When the Capitol was finished, John Brines and his wife travelled abroad in Italy and France, and he studied for six months in Paris. Then he established a studio in New York and there began creating sculpture of rare beauty. He died in 1905—of silicosis—at the age of forty-five.

Isaac Perry boasted of the carvings on the Eastern Stairway that "the work has been done with the greatest care and precision and is superior to any other granite work in this country."

As the skyscraper era in architecture dawned with the 20th Century, there was less and less demand for men who could carve stone on buildings.

Around 1952, when many renovations were underway at the Capitol, it was decided to finish up some ornamental strips of carving which, long ago, had been left incomplete in the Senate lobbies. But no one knew where to find carvers. The Lanzetta Marble Company, of Albany, had a contract for replacing marble floors. Daniel A. Lanzetta, head of that company, volunteered to search for some. He finally located three Italian carvers—two from New York, one from Wilkes-Barre, Pa. He learned that the youngest qualified stone carver in the United States was then past fifty years of age. The men came and completed the carving. They did it with pneumatic tools, and the dividing line can be clearly distinguished between their superficial work and the old work that was done with hammer and chisel.

*A gallery of carvings on Eastern Approach.
Brines roamed woodlands for real models
of native fauna. Across top of page
are an owl, raccoon, raven, and bob-cat.
Strong face of Negro (right) symbolizes
emancipation. Note broken link of chain.
Corbels of south colonnade are carved
to depict Industrial Arts, one being
the Mechanic, with tools of his trade.*

*Whimsicality crept into some carvings, giving rise
to a legend they were impromptu jests. Winking men are on
north portico. Woman thrusts out her tongue.*

12. OUT OF THE FLAMES

With morning light, March 29, 1911, this was the scene at west side of the Capitol. Fire had wrecked State Library and other parts of upper floors, but the Capitol had been saved. Old-fashioned fire engines belched more smoke than smoldering building itself. Alfred E. Smith, Robert Wagner, Sr., and Franklin D. Roosevelt were in the Legislature.

That night Louis McHenry Howe, a homely, asthmatic little man who was a demon for the news, worked very late in "Park Row," the third-floor press booths at the Capitol. He didn't mind the hour. As legislative correspondent for the *New York Telegram,* he was filing a story that was close to his heart.

The Democrats had won control of both houses of the Legislature for the 1911 session. By the nature of things, this automatically meant control by Tammany Hall. Louis Howe had been doing some part-time work for the reform Democrat, Thomas Mott Osborne, towards breaking the Tammany grip upstate. He knew it wasn't broken.

Soon after the 1911 session convened, an exciting thing happened, and it grew into the big political suspense-story of the winter. A revolt flared among a small coterie of Democratic legislators. Their boyish leader was a freshman Senator out of Dutchess County, and his name—soon hitting headlines from coast to coast—was Franklin D. Roosevelt. Brashly, this youth with the Harvard profile and the pince-nez glasses pitted himself against the seasoned key men of Tammany at Albany: Alfred E. Smith, majority leader of the Assembly, and Robert F. Wagner, president pro tem of the Senate. Political suicide, everyone said.

At that time, United States Senators were elected not by direct vote of the people, but by State Legislatures. New York had one to elect. The term of Chauncey M. Depew, Republican, would expire in March. Naturally the Legislature would choose a Democrat to succeed him. The Tammany boss, Charles F. Murphy, had picked his man—"Blue-Eyed Billy" Sheehan of Buffalo. Cynical newsmen, among them Louis Howe, poised their pencils to report the inevitable.

They as well as Murphy had reckoned without the new Senator from Dutchess. Franklin Roosevelt gathered a score of Democratic insurgents to stand with him and issued a manifesto that they would not support Sheehan and would not go along with any secret caucus. Their number was enough to block the election. The resulting deadlock went on for eleven weeks. Delightedly, Howe wrote: "It is the most humanly interesting political fight of many years."

Day by day, the Legislature caucused, getting nowhere. Tempers shortened. Roosevelt gained more recruits. Howe's editor asked him to interview the young upstart. The reporter came away convinced that "nothing but an accident could keep him from becoming President of the United States." This was the beginning of the fateful relationship between Roosevelt and Howe.

The night of Tuesday, March 28, the legislators held another fruitless caucus session in the Assembly Chamber. (Roosevelt and his group met at his Albany home, as usual.) Al Smith finally relieved Bob Wagner on the rostrum. The session dragged through four ballots until nearly 1 a.m. Weary members then retired to their hotel rooms. Two newsmen were still writing at 2:15 a.m.—Louis Howe, and Walter Arndt of the *New York Post*.

Suddenly, an Assembly clerk ran through the corridor shouting: "There is a fire in the Assembly library!"

The Assembly library was at some little distance to the rear of the Chamber, at one end of the State Library, which extended across the west side of the building on the third and fourth floors.

Here were two reporters in an enviable position to scoop all rivals. They dashed through the deserted Chamber and into the west corridor. In Howe's words:

"We looked in the room and saw the desk in the southwest corner ablaze. The fire at this time could have been easily put out with a pail or two of water. We searched in vain for anything to serve the purpose and finally decided to close the door and keep out the draft. The night watchman ran down stairs to sound the alarm, there being no alarms in the building."

Hindsight produced ample criticism of the lack of fire extinguishers; of the necessity for a watchman to go all the way down two flights and into the street to pull an alarm; and of the failure of anyone to think of telephoning the alarm. It was 25 minutes after the alarm that firemen were on the scene with their smoke-belching engines.

With stacks of paper and wooden shelves to feed upon—in a reputedly fireproof building—the flames grew prodigiously and exploded the windows and glass transom of the Assembly library before a single hose had been brought into play. With amazing speed, they spread along the corridor and into the State Library proper, as Howe and Arndt literally ran for safety to the Senate entrance. The two-story reading-room with its flanking book-stacks provided a perfect flue and the fuel to stoke it. Within 20 minutes the blaze was shooting high through the roof. Scorched sheets of paper out of the library were picked up six miles away, on the far side of the Hudson River, and kept as souvenirs.

Many people, answering the phone half-awake and being told "The Capitol is burning," thought it was a premature April Fool's joke. Such a one was Alfred E. Smith, but he rushed to a window and saw red clouds in the sky. Al never dressed so hastily. After fire-buffing for a time, he dropped in at a café that was doing a land-office business in the chilly March dawn. The proprietor wisecracked: "The Democrats were unable to take the Capitol away with them so they decided to burn it down." Smith mustered a hearty laugh.

The Great Gable stood out stark in silhouette against raging flames at height of the fire. It survived intact, as did the Great Western Staircase, although well smoked up. Gossip said blaze was started by cigar butt in a wastebasket. More likely cause was defective wiring of crude electric system.

The fire department strategy was to restrict the flames to the western side of the Capitol. If they ever got into one of the legislative chambers, the fire chief said afterwards, the entire building would have gone. Hoses were snaked up stairways, especially the Great Western. The latter, being directly across the corridor from the entrance to the State Library, was in particular jeopardy—but it also made a good vantage point for the firemen. Before the night was over, the skylight over the stairs caved in and showered them with glass, some of it dripping molten glass, like icicles. First accounts said this admired staircase, with all its expensive carvings, was ruined. Actually, aside from a thick layer of soot and a few nicks, it escaped damage miraculously.

The Senate Chamber never was seriously threatened. The Assembly Chamber was. At one point, flames crept into the loft above the ceiling and it began to burn. Firemen played high-pressure streams upon it from below, knocking out some of the papier mâché coffers. The fire in the attic was doused—not without some further insult to the forgotten Hunt murals.

The famous papier mâché panels, far from being inflammable, were fire-resistant—much more so than quartered oak would have been. And so the papier mâché, over which so much fuss had been made, was credited with saving the Assembly Chamber—hence, perhaps, the whole Capitol. (In the repair contract, 36 of the panels were replaced.)

Both legislative chambers suffered water damage. The well of the Assembly Chamber became a lake. A member standing on its brink jokingly proposed a bill to stock it with fish. The Axminster rugs were so sodden that stepping upon them was compared to walking on a bog. But the fire-fighters succeeded in confining the fire to the west section. Governor John A. Dix did business as usual next day in the Executive Chamber, bothered by nothing worse than a smoky smell.

In addition to the State Library and the bulk of its precious contents, many offices and committee-rooms were destroyed, among them the sanctum of the Speaker of the Assembly. The southwest corner tower fell in, and several portions of the roof. The superb triangular wall of the Great Gable came through intact.

The Capitol had seven night watchmen. A system of clock-punching on their rounds had been discarded not long before. One watchman was assigned exclusively to the State Library. He was Samuel J. Abbott, a Civil War veteran, 78 years old and growing feeble. During the fire, Capitol employees began asking one another: "Has anyone seen Abbott?" No one had. The old man was missing for two days. Then a clean-up squad found his charred body beneath rubbish in the fourth-floor corridor. Apparently he had been trying to reach a door when overcome by smoke.

Next morning the sun rose on a smoke-hazy, sleepy, and bewildered city. Just how much of the great building on the hill had been wrecked? Would it have to be entirely rebuilt?

The ruins smoldered, and fresh blazes broke out for days afterward. The building was placed under martial law and National Guardsmen patrolled with rifles.

The Million-Dollar Staircase was likened to a waterfall. Standing at the bottom, ruefully watching the cascade pouring down the steps, was Senator Franklin D. Roosevelt. A reporter sidled up to him and asked: "Do you think this will have any effect on the senatorial situation?"

"Not in the least," replied the insurgent leader. "The law says we have got to meet and vote at noon, anyway."

Albany's mayor offered the use of City Hall to the homeless Legislature. Uncomfortably, the Senate met in the city council chamber, the Assembly in the Supreme Court room. Al Smith made the motion to designate the City Hall as temporary Capitol of New York State, and it passed. Then the lawmakers rushed through an appropriation of $100,000 with which to start the clean-up.

Black headlines shouted across the nation: STATE CAPITOL SWEPT BY FLAMES. Early estimates of the damage ran as high as $7,000,000. Incidentally, the state carried no insurance on the building. After sober appraisal, the state architect set the actual building damage at $1,600,000. The reconstruction work, in the end, cost well over $2,000,000.

Far beyond any monetary yardstick was the grievous loss sustained by the State Library. The fire was called the greatest library disaster of modern times. Flames devoured 450,000 books and 270,000 manuscripts. Many of the sacrificial papers were historically priceless—such as early American colonial documents and the papers of statesmen. By luck and foresight, however, some of the rarest were saved. The Commissioner of Education, Dr. Andrew Sloan Draper—who had sounded repeated warnings of what a fire would do in the library stacks—had ordered certain items stored in a fireproof safe in the Regents suite on the first floor. Among these were original drafts of Lincoln's Emancipation Proclamation and Washington's Farewell Address; also the "spy papers" which Major John André had concealed in his boot when captured after his rendezvous with Benedict Arnold. The fire was held to the third floor and above.

Too long to be accommodated in this safe had been a dress sword that once belonged to George Washington. It went back into a library closet, and was bemoaned as lost in the fire. After several days, the sword was found, considerably damaged, beneath a thick pile of charred books.

The irony of it all was that the State Library was just marking time to move into its new quarters being readied in the State Education Building across the street. That building was completed the following year.

Generous offers of books to restore the State Library poured in. One such helping hand was extended by the Parliamentary Library in Ottawa—housed in a Thomas Fuller building.

Sardonic coincidence may be read into the fact that the three major governmental structures which Fuller designed (at least in part) on the American continent were visited by catastrophe. The San Francisco city hall was reduced to rubble by the earthquake of 1906. The main Parliament Building at Ottawa was burned in 1916 in a mysterious fire widely blamed on German sabotage, in which several people perished.

What caused the Capitol fire at Albany? The question never was answered with finality. Gossip whispered that some legislator, after the late caucus, dropped a cigar butt into a waste basket. But the caucus was held in the Assembly Chamber proper, not the Assembly library. Another rumor said a watchman had reported just recently that a light switch was heating up, and that nothing was done about it. This was not verified.

The likeliest explanation is that the electrical system was still functioning with the primitive wiring installed 25 years before when electric lights were a novelty. More than once, appropriations for new wiring had been refused. There was an immediate inspection of the wiring and it was found "very defective." Insulation was worn through; wires were laid against bare wood; telephone and bell-signal wires were found in contact with light wires. If a short circuit hadn't occurred, it was a miracle. Without waiting for legislative approval, Governor Dix ordered the old wires yanked out and an emergency wiring system put in. No time was wasted, either, in installing fire extinguishers and standpipes.

The fire had its political impact, too. Unquestionably, it hastened the end of the senatorial deadlock. The Legislature was cramped and unhappy in City Hall. It

The State Library then occupied top floors of Capitol's west side. It was principal victim of fire, losing many priceless documents. Stone-carving had extended into library, as photo illustrates. Next day, National Guardsmen put ruins under military law. The State Library was a sad sight.

wanted to go home while its own Chambers were put in order. Murphy, the Tammany sachem, caught a train for Albany. He proposed a compromise candidate, James A. O'Gorman, a Supreme Court justice. Most of the insurgents capitulated. O'Gorman was elected U. S. Senator on the 63rd caucus ballot, on March 31. Franklin D. Roosevelt, with two other hold-outs, stayed away from the caucus.

The Legislature then adjourned for two weeks. When it reconvened on April 17, the damaged corridors were boarded up and both Chambers were habitable, though Assemblymen complained that the very walls oozed dampness. Nearly every member was lacking his ready file of bills; they had been drenched and ruined the night of the fire. The first action in both Houses was to transfer the Capitol of New York State from City Hall back to where it belonged.

Always this Capitol, with its cavernous high-ceilinged rooms, had been vulnerable to the charge of waste space. In the reconstruction after the fire, a trend toward space-economy appeared. The area of the State Library (which would begin life anew in the Education Building) was converted into the Legislative Library, merging the hitherto separate Senate and Assembly libraries into one. But the room no longer was two stories high. Its handsome ceiling was also the floor of the fourth level, and offices went in above.

The Legislative Library introduced another fresh note into the heavily granitic building: it was the first all-marble room, and an almost effeminately dainty one. Frieze murals were painted around its walls by Will H. Low.

The only exterior change resulting from the calamity was the interpolation of three small dormers, which were not there before, on either flank of the Great Gable.

When Thomas E. Dewey became Governor in 1943, he desired some changes in the Executive suite. The legislators were willing to let him have them—on a quid pro quo basis. They badly needed additional office space. Thus was launched the most sweeping program of interior alterations since the Capitol was reared, going on for several years. The keynote was a more economical utilization of space in those outlandishly tall rooms. Mezzanines were introduced wholesale in the upper stories, and partitioned into new office suites. At that time, the skylights which had filtered at least some outer illumination into the stairwells of the Assembly and Senate staircases were eliminated; corridors of the fifth floor mezzanine were continued across them.

Now and again, when workmen took up their tools to cut an opening in a wall, they would be confronted by a formidable rampart of solid granite several feet thick. It would take days to drill through.

More than one architect or engineer who has worked on Capitol alterations has been heard to express the thought: "It cost the taxpayers plenty to build, but they sure got their money's worth!"

* * * * * * *

Down the decades, it has been a fashionable bromidiom to speak of New York's Capitol as being ugly and an "architectural monstrosity." This is a real injustice.

No one ever represented it to be a paragon of artistic structure. But it does have very considerable virtues, quite apart from the overall effect of "massiveness" with which even its severest critics have credited it. There is, perhaps, no other government building in America that is so architecturally *interesting*. The glib habit of disparagement is, no doubt, a vestigial echo of the general criticism that grew up during its protracted construction, when its cost was so far outstripping estimates and its design was being so much amended. The Capitol became a scapegoat then and never entirely lived it down. The time is long overdue for this building to be given its proper deserts.

The so-called "ceiling scandal" festered 10 years before its completion, and this added the element of alleged corruption to Capitol legendry. There is little doubt that the contractors made an exorbitant profit out of rebuilding the Assembly ceiling (not because papier mâché was used, but for other reasons)—yet the Legislature itself had left the door carelessly open. The truth is that not one person ever was convicted of dishonesty or graft in connection with the building's 30 years of construction. As in most large public projects of that era—and later—political patronage entered into the dispensing of jobs, but that was scarcely a punishable offense.

Admittedly, it is an architectural medley—with its two disparate varieties of Renaissance, its Richardsonian Romanesque, a smattering of Victorian Gothic, and overtones of the Moorish-Saracenic. Such a jumble of treatments may give the purist a case of aesthetic dyspepsia. But it is a stimulant to the interest of those who examine it with an open mind and some understanding of the process by which the styles got mixed. Certainly the building lacks unity and conventionality; but, by the same token, it also lacks monotony and boredom!

Those who planned it and promoted it were public-spirited, high-minded, conscientious men. They were not third-rate politicians dreaming up a boondoggle. They had a vision. They intended a majestic, inspired edifice that would shout to the world the wealth and importance of the Empire State. The time was ripe for such an enterprise, with the nation's industry expanding and its economy booming in the wake of the Civil War. Who worried about the money to push railroads to the Pacific Coast? Americans were thinking and talking big.

Considering the vicissitudes of its gestation, the wonder is that the New York Capitol turned out as well as it did. As was remarked at the outset, it probably is without peer as a building in which architecture and politics are intermingled. It stands unique as an essay in stone on the American democratic system, which is far from perfect but the best yet devised; in which the hopes and ideals always have a way of coming out on top of the mistakes and fumblings.

The men who conceived the new Capitol were resolved that it should be large enough and enduring enough to fulfill the needs of state government for generations to come. They wished it to have architectural distinction without being imitative of any other capitol yet built, state or national. They shopped a long time for a design that would meet their desires.

If they were vague in their ideas of what the architecture should be, this is not to be charged against them too heavily. Architecture in that post-war period was in a state of flux, groping for new directions. For several decades past, the Greek Revival had dominated the American scene structurally, with its marbled classicism, its pillars and pediments, until reaction had set in. Victorian Gothic spread from England as an antidote, but younger architects were rebelling against that, too. It took courage and much originality to break the bonds in which they had been tightly schooled.

The sudden renown which came to Thomas Fuller for his design of the Canadian Parliament Buildings made it inevitable that special attention would be paid to the designs he submitted in competition for the Albany Capitol. Still, he had to re-do them again and again before the state awarded him the commission. The Capitol planners were amateurs of architecture, and yet Fuller had to meet certain preconceived ideas in his winning design. By the time the basic faults were realized—the open central court, the prodigality of space, the lack of a noble main-floor rotunda, the inconvenience of locating the legislative chambers remotely on the third floor— it was too late to mend them without tearing down what had been built and starting over. It was also much too late to keep the cost within the legislated bounds of $4,000,000 which the originators had naively imagined would cover the cost of such a building.

At long last the State Capitol will be viewed in perspective, as architects intended it. Demolition for the South Mall had opened things up enough to permit this photograph of distinctive south façade, hitherto tightly hedged in by rows of decaying buildings. Richardson left his imprint especially upon this face. Plan calls for a new stairway to enter here from the Mall.

The architects who were employed to remedy the situation did the best they could under the circumstances. They were not nobodies. Richardson and Eidlitz were among the finest architects in the United States. Richardson, in fact, became the recognized leader of a whole new school of the young rebels. Eidlitz was trying to do something different and imaginative with the Victorian Gothic. These were modern architects of their time. They were also very courageous architects, to undertake the salvation of this building by modifying its style after it was half-done, in the face of the outraged protests of the tradition-bound majority of their profession. They worked hard, and often at their own financial sacrifice, to make it a building of some artistic distinction, if not perfection. And they succeeded, to a surprising degree.

Those architects expected the Capitol to be surrounded by spacious, well-tended grounds. This was part of the plan—to demolish the already degenerating residential blocks adjacent, so that spectators might stand off and appreciate its façades from a little distance, as they might a painting in a gallery. Frederick Law Olmsted, the top-ranking landscape architect who was allied with them, had worked out an elaborate landscaping plan. It never materialized. The Capitol was left hemmed in by elderly row-houses. It is no exaggeration to say that the building never was rightly seen—until recent time.

A full century after the preliminary legislation that set it going, the New York Capitol found itself the pivot of a far greater development than was envisioned by its early sponsors in their most optimistic moments. Like the elder statesman, mellow in years and wisdom, it was elected to preside at the head of the South Mall—the future working heart of New York State government.

The dramatic South Mall project was set in motion in 1962 by Governor Nelson Rockefeller and the Legislature. The city of Albany entered into a long-range cooperative program with the state, with a view to converting itself into one of the more beautiful of American capitals.

A temporary State Commission on the Capital City was established, its membership balanced between government officials and private citizens, with Lieutenant Governor Malcolm Wilson as chairman. Under its supervision, the new state structures were to be integrated with a general renewal plan for the city as a whole. The Commission recommended that the focus of future state construction be redirected from peripheral areas of the city towards downtown Albany.

During 1963, the clearing away of solid city blocks of deteriorated buildings was well advanced in a broad swath of 98 acres, extending a half-mile southward from the Capitol building. In the corridor thus opened, a splendid concourse would take form along an axis of reflecting pools and fountains. Flanking this would evolve a complex of governmental buildings, of advanced architectural style. Among them were envisioned tall, slender office buildings, as well as varied structures to contain an auditorium, the State Library, State Museum, and State Archives. Separate office buildings for both the Senate and the Assembly are contemplated.

Facing the granitic Richardsonian ramparts of the Capitol from the far end of the South Mall would stand an Arch of Freedom, arresting in design. Another broad external flight of stairs was to be added, bridging State Street and affording access direct from the Mall into the second floor of the Capitol. The massy old building itself will be sanded to something like its original whiteness.

The South Mall will place the Capitol in true perspective for the first time since it was built. There it will loom in sharp but comfortable contrast to the austere lines of the modern buildings—a nostalgic reminder of a bygone era and other tastes in architecture, but still an impressive symbol of the "resources, the power and the grandeur of the Empire State of the Union."

The eventful years of a century
wheeled past and the Capitol
stood as sturdily as when built.
Once again a dream took shape.
The dream, translated to reality,
would be named the South Mall.
A pulsing heart of government, it
was conceived too as an asset
to a more beautiful capital city.
Far from becoming a wall-flower,
the massive old Capitol building
was assigned to a leading role
in the unfolding new drama.
In the plan for the South Mall,
it faces down a grand concourse and
a series of reflecting pools.
Office structures stand sentinel
along each side of the concourse.
Above drawing looks south along
Mall, Arch of Freedom at far end.

ACKNOWLEDGMENTS

Numerous individuals were helpful in the research for this book, and a few in the loan of rare pictorial material. The author particularly tenders his gratitude to the following:

Martin H. Bush, Syracuse, who laid the groundwork by collecting many source documents and photographs; Alfred H. Hallenbeck, building superintendent, State Capitol; William S. King, former clerk of the Senate for twenty years; Kenneth De Kay, associate director, Office of Legislative Research; Norman S. Rice, curator, Albany Institute of History and Art; Thomas G. Fuller, Ottawa, Ontario, grandson of Thomas Fuller, first architect of the Capitol; Mrs. Charles S. Hamlin, Albany, daughter of John V. L. Pruyn, member of the original New Capitol Commission; Mrs. William G. Phelps, Jr., Binghamton, granddaughter of Isaac G. Perry, last architect of the Capitol; Mrs. Miriam Albee Clausen, Albany, granddaughter of Louis J. Hinton, designer and foreman of carvers on the Western Staircase; Mrs. Harold Chadderdon, Catskill, daughter of Otto Baumgartel, sculptor for the Western Staircase; Mrs. Gertrude Arenholz, Poughkeepsie, daughter of Killian Drabold, stone-carver on the Western Staircase; Mrs. Carl Koechlin, Athens, N. Y.; Mr. and Mrs. Edward A. Marx, Albany; Mr. and Mrs. Drew W. Standrod, Albany; William J. Desmond, long-time Capitol guard; Thomas Bartlow, former Capitol guide; Vincent deP. Martin, assistant to the chief architect, and various others of the State Architect's staff too many to name; the staff of the New York State Library for assembling the State Capitol Collection, which will be kept as such in the future; the Library of Congress; and the Regents of the University of the State of New York. For the use of photographs, particular thanks go to the New York Public Library, New York City; the Albany Institute of History and Art; the Franklin D. Roosevelt Memorial Library at Hyde Park, N. Y.; the Museum of Fine Arts, Boston, Mass.; the Public Archives of Canada, Ottawa, Ontario; Morris Gerber, the Gerber Collection, Albany; Dick Farr, New York State Department of Education.

Additional copies at $1.00 apiece may be obtained by writing to the Gift and Exchange Section, New York State Library, Albany, New York. Payment is required with order. Checks and money orders should be made payable to the New York State Education Department.